Because we live in a world that constantly seeks to define who we are, we need to be equipped to combat the enemy's lies and declare God's truth over our lives. In *Beautifully Designed*, Ashley cuts straight through the lies many women face and shows what God's Word has to say about our worth and identity. This book is a must-have for those who seek to persevere in life and discover who they are in Christ.

~ **Alisa Nicaud,** founder of FlourishingToday.com

Grab your seat belt and hold on tight, because *Beautifully Designed* will propel you straight toward Jesus and your true identity! How many times have you looked in the mirror and labeled yourself as ugly, fat, or worthless? Ashley understands what it's like to live this way, because she's been there. With a comforting and highly relatable writing style, she champions readers to grab hold of their true identity as a daughter of God. This is a journey you don't want to miss!

~ **Kristi Woods,** author, speaker, blogger at KristiWoods.net

I don't know a woman who *can't* relate to Ashley's story! Her courageous approach to helping women discover their identity and value is truly a gift to all who come across her work. I distinctly remember my own journey of discovering my identity and how difficult it was to navigate. There are so many women who have yet to take this journey and need to read *Beautifully Designed*. If you struggle with comparison, unmet ideals, depression, shame, anxiety, or simply feel like you don't measure up, I encourage you to read this book immediately and be set free!

~ **Jenny Donnelly,** co-pastor of The Collective Church (Portland, Oregon), author, blogger at JennyToday.com

Beautifully Designed is perfect for the modern woman who lives in a world of comparison. Ashley Shepherd is a gifted teacher; her words and real-life stories will touch your heart and help you believe you can be and do more. This book is practical, down-to-earth, and an answer to prayer for anyone searching for their true identity in a world of confusion and chaos.

~ **Diane McDaniel,** pastor at Bethel Dallas, entrepreneur, inspirational speaker, and writer

To receive, believe, and understand that they are beautifully designed does not come easily for many women. In this book, Ashley invites you on a journey to wholeness. She shares her own life stories in an engaging fashion with a raw vulnerability that leaves you feeling as though you are in her living room having a one-on-one conversation. At the center of this conversation is the very real story of a God who desires to meet you right where you are and redefine your life so you can see His original design and purpose. So, as Ashley says, "grab a blanket and find a comfortable chair or spot on the couch" and allow God to heal your heart to reveal your beautiful design.

~ **Ruth Hendrickson,** pastor, conference speaker, ministry trainer, counselor;
Ruth Hendrickson Ministries

As a campus minister, I regularly work with college students who are unsure of their identity and could greatly benefit from *Beautifully Designed*. I love the way Ashley blends biblical examples with her own story, showing us what it looks like to go from bondage to freedom as we exchange negative labels for the truth of who God says we are.

~ **Allison Abey,** campus staff minister with Athletes InterVarsity Christian Fellowship at The College of New Jersey

Beautifully DESIGNED

Abandon Labels, Discover God's Truth

Alice,

You are beautifully designed. Never forget how loved you are!

Ashley Shepherd

BATTLE GROUND
creative

Beautifully Designed

Copyright © 2017 by Ashley Shepherd
All rights reserved.

Published in Houston, Texas, by Battle Ground Creative
First Edition

softcover: 978-1-947554-91-7
ebook: 978-1-947554-92-4
RELIGION / Christian Life / Spiritual Growth

Battle Ground Creative is a publishing company with an emphasis on helping first-time authors find their voice. Named after an obscure city in Washington State, we currently operate offices in Houston, Texas, and Princeton, New Jersey. For a complete title list and bulk order information, please visit www.battle-groundcreative.com.

Unless otherwise noted, scripture quotations are taken from THE HOLY BIBLE, NEW INTERNATIONAL VERSION®, NIV® Copyright © 1973, 1978, 1984, 2011 by Biblica, Inc.® Used by permission. All rights reserved worldwide.

Scriptures marked "ESV" are taken from The ESV® Bible (The Holy Bible, English Standard Version®), copyright © 2001 by Crossway, a publishing ministry of Good News Publishers. Used by permission. All rights reserved.

Scriptures marked "NLT" are taken from the Holy Bible, New Living Translation, copyright © 1996, 2004, 2007 by Tyndale House Foundation. Used by permission of Tyndale House Publishers, Inc., Carol Stream, Illinois 60188. All rights reserved.

Scriptures marked "The Message" are taken from The Message. Copyright © 1993, 1994, 1995, 1996, 2000, 2001, 2002. Used by permission of NavPress Publishing Group.

Senior copyeditor: Jared Stump
Cover design: Amber Bell
Cover image: Lightstock
Author photo: Lauren Reeves
Interior design and typeset: Katherine Lloyd

Printed in the United States of America

> "I learned more about Christianity from my mother than from all of the theologians in England."
>
> —John Wesley

This book is dedicated to my beautiful mom, Teresa Loveday. She not only told me about Jesus Christ when I was a young girl, she has modeled what it looks like to live a life in obedience to Him. This ripple effect was begun by her mother, Deanna Barker, who is now with Jesus. These women have helped me know that who I am in Christ is the only thing that truly matters. I am grateful that I can continue this legacy with my family and to every woman I meet through my ministry and writing this book.

I want to thank my sister, Keeli Boyce. She came up with the name *Beautifully Designed* and has supported me my entire life. Keeli, you are an inspiration to me and I love raising our village together.

I also want to thank my grandmother, Reba Loveday, for continually praying God's Word over me and my family.

A huge thank you to my mother-in-love, Amy Shepherd, for teaching her family to love Jesus Christ above all, and for loving me like a daughter.

Each of our lives create a ripple effect in the lives of others. I pray that this book takes you on a journey where you begin creating a legacy of strong women who rest their identity in Jesus Christ. This ripple effect will last for generations and echo into eternity.

Contents

Foreword by Angie Smith xi

Introduction – Meet Ashley 1

Chapter 1 **You Have Been Labeled** 5

Chapter 2 **Words** 11

Chapter 3 **Self-Image** 25

Chapter 4 **Failure** 37

Chapter 5 **Shame** 55

Chapter 6 **People-Pleasing** 71

Chapter 7 **Self-Worth** 89

Chapter 8 **Daughter** 103

Next Steps 119

Connect with Us 125

Bring Ashley to Your Community 127

About the Author 129

Foreword

by Angie Smith

I met Ashley in a strange, yet wonderful way. She was leading my Bible study, *Seamless*, for a small group of women online. By "small," I mean 10,000 women. I was absolutely blown away that someone was able to host and lead a group of that size, which made me curious to discover who she was.

When we first spoke, Ashley told me she had only expected a few dozen women to join her online study. She was just as shocked as I was when there ended up being several thousand women in the Bible study. When I met Ashley in person, I understood why she has this effect on people. Within minutes we were knee-deep in conversation that far surpassed the typical "Isn't the weather nice!" small talk. She told me about her incredible journey to living a healthier life and I just plain liked her from the very beginning.

The way Ashley invited me into her story made me realize why so many women admire and appreciate her. She glows with the love of Jesus and is the perfect combination of kindness, welcoming, and depth. When she told me that she wanted to share her story to encourage other women, I was so excited and encouraged her to do so.

I'm grateful for the opportunity to be a small part of Ashley's story. I have no doubt that as you read this book, you will feel as though Ashley is sitting right next to you. I am confident that you'll be able to find pieces of your own story and be encouraged as you discover that you are beautifully designed.

—Angie Smith
Bestselling Author of *Seamless* and *What Women Fear*
Nashville, TN

Introduction

Meet Ashley

If you are like me, you may have picked up this book and wondered how you would make time to read it. I know your schedule and to-do list may be pulling you in many different directions, but I believe this book will lead you straight to the One who not only designed you, but will give you the peace you long for in your heart.

As women, we often wear many hats, and there are many parts of our lives we try to hide. There are some things we "just don't talk about" as we strive to maintain appearances and ensure that our lives remain picture-perfect from the outside. Whether you are a wife, mother, grandmother, or student, I think you'll be able to relate to this feeling. There is enormous pressure on women today, and I have seen it start as early as junior high and even elementary school. At times, there are parts of our hearts that we bury and don't share with anyone, not even our significant other or closest friends.

Place your hand on your heart. Can you feel and hear your heart beat? If you are still breathing, you have a specific purpose and call on your life. You were not designed to just barely "make it" through life; you were not created to hide or feel invisible. It is time for you to rise up, tap into the life and strength that God offers, and live out your destiny!

I wish you were in my living room, sitting across from me, so I could look you in the eyes and express my heart to you on a deeper level. Since that isn't possible, I invite you to grab a blanket and find a comfortable chair or spot on the couch. Get cozy as we begin this journey together. It is my prayer that, by the time you reach the end of this book, you will know how *loved* and how *beautiful* you are.

Your calendar and life may already be full, but I'd like to ask you to commit to this book from beginning to end. This is a journey we're on together, a journey to discover where our true identity lies. It's not in the labels that are put on us—or the labels we put on ourselves. It's not in our past mistakes or failures or even our present ones. It's not in our perfect church attendance or morality. Our identity is something much deeper, something that we can only find in Christ. We were created by God and for God; each of us has a Creator and a Redeemer who desires to have a close relationship with us.

I hope you are able to gather some of your girlfriends and dive into this book together. On this journey, we will smile together, laugh together, and possibly even cry together, but I hope that, ultimately, each of us hears God's still small voice whisper to our hearts as I share stories from both the Scriptures and my own personal journey.

As you read this book, you will find prayer prompts and space for you to journal. I invite you to take the time to encounter God and allow Him to personalize the truths He speaks to your heart in each chapter. You may not be able to relate to every label we discuss in this book, but I guarantee you someone you know has struggled with it or currently is struggling with a specific one. At the end of each chapter, there will be an opportunity to replace the negative labels that may have stuck to you with the only truth there is: God's word and what He says about you.

Before we dive in, let me tell you a little about myself. I grew up as a preacher's kid in Eastern Tennessee. My parents (Kent and Teresa Loveday) raised my sister, Keeli, and me in a positive, encouraging, and loving environment. They supported us as we pursued basketball, ballet, acting, and other silly ventures. There has never been a time when I cannot simply pick up the phone to call my mom or dad and glean from their wisdom.

Meet Ashley

The summer before my sophomore year of college, I met the man who would become my husband. Although I went on to graduate with a bachelor's degree, I knew that God had me at Middle Tennessee State University to meet Ryan Shepherd. I ended up graduating in 2004 with two degrees—journalism and Mrs., if you know what I mean. We were married the following year and are now raising our two boys, Wilson and Levi, in the beautiful Smoky Mountains where I grew up. My husband is a pilot and we are both entrepreneurs who run a home-based business together, which gives us freedom and flexibility to prioritize our family.

Though my life may seem picture-perfect from the outside, I have been through my share of tough times as most of us have. I've struggled with depression and had seasons where I wasn't sure of my identity. If we're honest, I believe all women experience these seasons; we just never talk about them. I'm not sure why this is, but I think it's because we often think we are the only ones who struggle and everyone else's lives are truly as perfect as they appear from the outside and on social media, so we leave our masks on in an exhausting attempt to prove to the world that we've got it together.

In the fall of 2015, I was participating in an amazing study by Angie Smith called "Seamless" that goes through the entire Bible as one complete story. My friend and I enjoyed it so much that we thought it would be fun to do the study online for our friends who live out of town. We thought we would gather 100 women, but God had other plans. Within four weeks, we had 9,000 women participating in the study through our Facebook group, which we called "Beautifully Designed."

I was blown away by the response and from the outside, it may have appeared that I was "living the dream." However, at the same time, there were many fears and insecurities creeping in beneath the surface. People were beginning to look up to me as a sort of "spiritual leader," but I knew I was an imperfect, broken mom who struggled to read her Bible on a daily basis.

It was not long before I realized that these women were craving community, with thousands of new members joining the group each day. God began to connect the dots, and it wasn't long before more than 17,000 women had joined the Beautifully Designed community. Today, we regularly join together to pray, study the Scriptures, and give one another hope as each woman discovers her true identity in Christ. God is doing something amongst this group, and it is very exciting to be right in the middle of it!

Beautifully Designed is a community that God has brought together for the sole purpose of helping women discover their true identity in Him, which I have found is much easier in community. This book is an expression of my heart for women to discover who they are in Christ which I pray will encourage you to rise above the noise of this world and begin following after the One who beautifully designed you.

No matter where you find yourself in life, no matter what challenges you have faced and what obstacles you have overcome, there is a Savior who is ready to take you in His arms and remind you how loved you truly are. Close your eyes, take a deep breath, and get ready as we begin this journey together.

—Ashley Shepherd
Maryville, TN
Summer, 2017

Chapter 1

You Have Been Labeled

label
- [ley-*buh* l]

noun
1. a small piece of paper, fabric, plastic, or similar material attached to an object and giving information about it.

While doing laundry one morning, I pulled my favorite shirt out of the dryer—an oversized tee with the Chicago Cubs logo across the front. It had already been one of "those" mornings, and I had decided that my attire for the day would consist of leggings and my oversized shirt, which I put on before I had even finished removing the rest of the clothes from the dryer.

Moments later, when I looked in the mirror, I nearly lost it. A white, sticky residue was stuck to the fabric! I stared blankly into the mirror for a bit, wondering what this could be. It was then that I remembered that I had worn a name tag at an event the night before and, apparently, had never taken it off. This label had come off in the wash and left a sticky residue in its place. Taking a deep breath, I changed shirts and told myself I would deal with it later.

Later that night, I tried peeling the sticky residue off my favorite shirt. This only made me more frustrated, as using my fingernail to scratch off the label only created a larger mess. In the moment, I couldn't tell if I was more irritated by the ruined shirt or the fact that I had forgotten to remove the label before putting my shirt in the wash.

During this particular week, it seemed that I was getting myself into several "sticky" situations that left me feeling overwhelmed. In my life, I wear multiple hats. I'm the mother of two young boys (Wilson and Levi) who seem to always be sticky. (Why is that, anyway?) I'm also a wife to Ryan, I work from home, lead a ministry called Beautifully Designed, and am a friend to many. I sometimes feel like I have several plates spinning at once with no place to land, and this night was no exception as I found myself in a sticky situation.

Have you ever felt like you have so much going on that you can't fully give your all to any one thing or be fully present for your family? I don't always feel this way, but I did on this particular evening. All I wanted to do was hide inside my comfy shirt and leggings and have a good cry, but even my shirt was a total disaster!

My feet came to a rest at the foot of the bed as I slid beneath the covers, but my mind continued to race at full speed as my head hit the pillow. I began replaying the events of the day in my mind: working, household chores, running errands, cooking dinner, and rushing the kids to bed so the house would be quiet and I could squeeze in a few more tasks since Ryan was out of town. I couldn't help but think about the things I didn't do, the things I shouldn't have said. On top of all this, my body was exhausted. I felt like I had been spinning my wheels all day, yet, I still felt like a failure. It wasn't one big thing that made me feel this way but 467 different scenarios swirling in my mind.

As I lay in bed, I realized that my frustration was not just about my ruined shirt. In reality, it was about something much deeper. There wasn't just a sticky label on my shirt but labels I had stuck to myself and never taken off, some of which I had been carrying for most of my life. In my mind, the label of "Ashley Shepherd" did not reflect my true identity in Christ but brought to mind words like *dumb*, *not enough*, and even *failure*. But why is this the case?

I have struggled for years with insecurities and the general feeling that I am "not enough." I can recall this beginning as early as the age of six when I would tell myself how stupid I was on a regular basis.

I was born six weeks early and was still tiny as a young girl. I struggled in school and felt as though I always had to work extra hard to accomplish things. I have memories of my teachers telling my mom I should be held back instead of advancing to the next grade. I have vivid memories of one occasion, as my mom and I were driving down the road, when I looked at her and asked if I would ever make it out of first grade. I remember nights when I would write "I am stupid" on pieces of paper and hide them under my pillow, so my mom wouldn't find them.

I realize now that there was no reason for me to ever think that about myself. I may have done stupid things from time to time, but that didn't make *me* stupid. There's a huge difference, and I have found that when we make mistakes, there are always "voices" (whether the voices of others or the enemy of our souls) to tell us that *we* are stupid and *we* are a mistake when that is *not* what God says about us!

Now that I am a mother to two boys, I would be heartbroken if I ever ran across a note that they wrote calling themselves stupid. I had great parents who were very supportive, introduced me to Jesus, and spoke life into me in the midst of my insecurities. Still, there were many times when I felt lost and wanted to hide. This began in my childhood and has followed me into adulthood. As I lay in bed thinking about my ruined shirt, I began to relive those memories and emotions from when I was six years old. As I got out of bed to look for my Bible, I felt like I was that little girl again, the girl who always felt like she had to "catch up."

Grabbing my Bible, I paused and asked myself a simple, yet daunting question. *Who am I?* I felt like I was undergoing an identity crisis. The desire to hide began to overwhelm me yet again as I wrestled with my perceived failures. *If I can just curl up on the couch, maybe my husband won't notice that I didn't do the dishes. Maybe my kids won't notice that I never put their clothes away. Maybe my gym trainer won't notice I've been absent for two weeks. Maybe my friends won't notice that I haven't been present in their lives—because my own was leaving me feeling paralyzed. Maybe I can make myself invisible just for a little while, so I won't have to be "enough" for everyone else, and I can just be me.*

Instead of opening up a package of Oreos, I sought refuge in the Word of God. While I don't recall what Scriptures I read that night, I remember my heart rate slowing to the point that I was able to fall asleep.

The next morning the sun was just peeking through the window as my feet hit the floor. I quickly jumped into my usual routine but couldn't stop thinking about labels. Throughout the day, I began to write down each thought I had about myself. The first was "tired." Even though I had slept all night, one look at my calendar exhausted me. The second was "dumb," because I couldn't answer my son's math problem. (I mean, when did third grade get so hard?!) As I looked at the sheet of paper, I realized those were the labels I was wearing—and that I was the one who had put them there.

Suddenly, it all began to make sense. The reason why the label on my favorite shirt frustrated me so much was about something much deeper than a ruined shirt. My reaction on the surface revealed something about how I saw myself on the inside. Because I viewed myself as "dumb," I was way too hard on myself over an innocent mistake. Because I viewed myself as "tired," I was even tougher on myself, because it didn't feel like I even had time to fix my mistake.

Throughout the morning, I continued to write down each thought I had about myself. By lunch, I was in tears as I realized how many labels I had attached to myself and how they were leaving a sticky residue on my heart and soul. I knew this was *not* who God created me to be, but my question from the night before remained—*Who am I?*

TAKE A DEEP BREATH

Have you ever asked yourself a similar question?

Who am I?

It's a question that haunts so many of us.

Though I know the truth of what God says about me in my *head*, I don't always live with an awareness of this in my *heart*. This is why we must remember the truth about who God says we are! This isn't just something you need once a day in your quiet time but a moment-by-moment reminder throughout the day. I don't just need to read in the Scriptures about who God says I am; I need to allow that reality to sink deep into my heart.

Imagine I am sitting across from you looking into your eyes. Now, take a deep breath. Grab your Bible and a pen. You may want to curl up under your covers and hide, but instead, I encourage you to allow Jesus to hide you in His arms.

Do you feel as though you have been labeled? Are those labels that are attached to you positive or negative?

What are some of the labels that have attached themselves to your heart? (If you're not sure, ask God to show you!)

Do you allow negative self-talk and the opinions of others to dictate how you feel or who you are? If so, are you ready to replace those lies with truth? Spend a few minutes in prayer asking God to reveal your true identity and remove the negative labels that have gotten in the way.

Chapter 2

Words

word
- [wurd]

noun
1. a single distinct meaningful element of speech or writing, used with others (or sometimes alone) to form a sentence and typically shown with a space on either side when written or printed.

Although I loved sports growing up, I was never exceptionally good at any of them. I had abandoned cheerleading for basketball, but at the end of the day, I was really only on the team because I wanted to hang out with my girls. I was an average student from an academic standpoint but a social butterfly who loved meeting new people.

As my senior year of high school came to a close, I met with my guidance counselor to discuss choosing a major for college. Unfortunately, "people" wasn't a topic I could major in, so I was unsure of what to put on my application for Middle Tennessee State University (MTSU).

Looking me in the eyes, my guidance counselor said, "You are an awesome writer. Have you considered journalism?" I nearly fell out of my chair. I loved writing but was shocked that someone had noticed. I had spent so much of my life focusing on what I *wasn't* good at that I overlooked my love of writing. The words of my guidance counselor gave me a newfound confidence. He had noticed a gift in me that had been lost in a sea of negativity and self-doubt.

The following fall, I began my freshmen year at MTSU where I majored in journalism. A year had passed, but my heart was still holding onto the words of my guidance counselor.

Words have unbelievable power, and hearing someone tell me I was "awesome" at something filled my heart with hope. For the first time in my life, I actually felt like I had a shot at being successful in at least one area. So, for the next four years, I held onto the words of my guidance counselor with every paper I turned in, secretly praying that he was right. I had to pray, because there were so many other words that floated across my mind. These words sounded nothing like "awesome" and threatened to squash the hope that I could be successful. "Defeated," "exhausted," and "not enough" were a few of the words I felt were most true. I often found myself tempted to come into agreement with these words and allow them to define my life, but from time to time, I thought back to that day in my high school guidance counselor's office. My heart would skip a beat as I realized there were people out there that believed the opposite of the narrative that seemed to play in my head on repeat.

Who is one person who has played the role of an encourager in your life? How did they encourage you?

How did it make you feel to know someone believed in you?

No matter what stage of life you find yourself in—student, young mom, parent of teenagers, or a grandmother—you likely play many roles and are many things to different people. As you move through life, these roles change. You will eventually graduate college, your kids will grow up; no season of life lasts forever. As your roles change, so do the voices in your head and the words you believe about yourself. It can be your own thoughts, the opinions of others, or comparing yourselves to someone's social media highlight reel late at night. The bottom line is there are words that enter our minds and, if we're not careful, these words can stick to our hearts and become our identity rather than the truth of who God says we are.

This is very important, because the words that we believe about ourselves have the power to change the way we see ourselves, the way we interact with others—even the way we view God! This is true in both a positive and negative sense. When we listen to the words the enemy speaks to our heart, they have the power to diminish the way we view ourselves and the way we view God. However, when we choose to listen to who God says we are, He begins to shape and form us into the people He has called us to be. We cannot step into our true identity as daughters of the King while we are still believing the lies of the enemy!

Some of you grew up in an environment where you had no one speaking words of life and hope to your heart. It may not have necessarily been a toxic environment; you just had no one to lead you into your true identity in Christ, no one who you knew believed in you that you could go to with any issue you were facing.

No matter how positive or negative your upbringing was, I believe deep down we all share a common desire for words of encouragement—especially in a culture that works overtime to shame and discourage women.

I grew up in a positive environment with a loving and supporting family. I even had people around me, such as my guidance counselor at MTSU, who encouraged me along the way. But even with all of this love and support, I still experienced an identity crisis after leaving college and getting married. I felt lost, weighed down by lies, and not sure of my purpose in life.

I think most all women have struggled with similar feelings at some point in their lives. It's so much easier to believe lies than it is to believe the affirmation that comes our way. I don't know why this is the case, but it seems as though a woman can receive dozens of compliments, yet the one critical remark she receives is what will stick with her. At least, that has been my experience.

One day, as I was thinking about this, I grew curious if any other women felt the same way. This curiosity got the best of me, and I ended up posting a status on Facebook that read: "Ladies, I am working on a project and would love your help. What is one 'label' you have allowed to attach itself to you and define who you are?" I then offered some examples, both positive and negative: *Beautiful, powerful, tired, defeated, fat, failure.*

Within twenty-four hours, several hundred women had listed the labels that define them. A few examples include: *stupid, ugly, weak, lazy, insignificant, disappointment, inconsistent, unworthy, worthless, weird, quitter, workaholic, not wanted, not enough, broken, lacking, unloved, and just a mom.*

Tears began to well up in my eyes as I read these words, the vast majority of which were negative. One woman had gone as far as to label herself as "a waste of space." All I wanted to do was drive over to these women's houses and hug them. What was even more shocking was hearing the words some of my *friends* spoke over their lives. *I never knew they thought about themselves that way*, I thought to myself. But the reality was, I, too, had lived most of my life believing the same things.

Many of us don't recognize that the negative words that cross our minds throughout the day are actually labels. When we don't counteract these labels by replacing them with God's truth, we end up buying into them as if they are our true, unchangeable identity.

It can begin with hearing someone say "you're stupid" (or telling yourself that you're stupid). If you continue to meditate on this false label and don't let the truth of who God says you are replace it, it won't be long before you buy into this label and actually convince yourself that you are stupid.

My simple experiment left me with a great responsibility. I knew I had to come alongside these women, so we could face our giants together. God then showed me that this was the reason why I had gone through so many seasons of depression and feeling unsure of my true identity. He didn't allow me to go through those things because He wanted me to suffer, but because He knew it would help me learn to persevere and help others who are struggling. Because I have been through these things and overcome them, I am able to help other women realize that they, too, can overcome through Jesus Christ if they choose to fight the battle to abandon their labels and discover the truth of who God says they are.

I realized that, for most of these women, there was a day when these words were spoken to them, shouted at them, or mentally whispered to their hearts. The stickiness of these words had left not only a residue, but a wound on their hearts. Left unhealed, those wounds would continue to hurt. I also realized that these hurts are not casual conversation topics. Most women never talk about the negative words they have believed about themselves, and even when they do, they don't often realize where these wounds came from or how to address them.

If you look up John 10:10 in the Bible, you will see that we have an enemy who seeks to steal, kill, and destroy. If you have a relationship with Jesus, the enemy cannot steal that from you. However, he can attempt to steal your joy, your sense of security, and your self-worth. One of the greatest schemes of the enemy to distract women from God's purpose for their lives is to label them with lies that, over time, begin to define them and destroy the lives God intended them to live. Once these labels are attached, the enemy's goal is to make sure your words, actions, and life reflect that label, rather than the truth of who God says you are.

What are the words you whisper to yourself most often? (If you are unsure of what to write down, what are the first words that come to mind when you look at yourself in the mirror?)

....
....
....

Do these words reveal any new labels that you did not previously realize are attached to you?

....
....

If I listed all of the words I have allowed the enemy to whisper to me, this book would look more like an encyclopedia! There have been days when I felt completely overwhelmed by the amount of words that made their way into my mind; they created a weight on my heart that began to pull me down and send me into hiding.

One day, as I was dropping Wilson off at his preschool, another mom invited me to her small group. The only thing I could think of in response was, *why in the world would she want to invite me?* My goal was to get my child into class as quickly as possible, so I could go back into hiding until it was time to pick him up. The last thing I wanted to do was spend time with other women who might see my flaws. I didn't want to come out of hiding even though that was where my healing was. I even had long, janky (yes, that is a word in the South!) bangs that made it difficult for anyone to look me in the eyes. I wasn't trying to go back to 1989 or be a trendsetter; I was simply trying to hide. I thought if I stayed in the background, I would become invisible, and no one would notice my imperfections. I was overweight at the time and walked around feeling defeated most days. It wasn't just the bangs; I would also hide behind big sweaters which I often wore—even when it was eighty degrees outside.

Words

As I sat in the car later that morning, I wrestled in my mind with whether or not I would take the woman up on her offer to attend her small group. My insecurities said "no," but my desire to connect with other women screamed "YES!"

What you believe about yourself matters. Your words matter and can either bring life or death (Proverbs 18:21), and this includes the words you speak to yourself or allow the enemy to speak to you. In this season of my life, the words I was believing were bringing death to my joy, confidence, and sense of hope. I could no longer hear the word "awesome" that was spoken to me by my guidance counselor years before; it had been clouded by the word "inadequate" and many more negative words. I felt lost, unsure of who I was. The enemy knew that each negative word whispered to my heart chipped away at the one thing that gave me a lasting sense of purpose: my identity in Christ.

Have you ever felt lost or unsure of your identity? Describe a time when you felt this way.

My sister, Keeli, had a tangible experience that illustrates how I felt quite well. She called me in a frenzy one afternoon and told me that her credit card company was investigating her for allegedly committing fraud against herself. Yes, you read that correctly! She had seen charges show up on her statement for things she didn't order. After reporting them, she thought all was well until the call came from her credit card company.

Apparently, someone had gotten a hold of Keeli's credit card information, created a fraudulent PayPal account in her name, bought several things online, had them shipped to her house, and then picked the packages up from her house before she noticed they were there.

Her credit card company told her they had to launch an investigation, because they didn't know if someone else was behind this or if she was trying to get away with not paying for things she had ordered. Keeli began to panic at the thought that someone was watching her house to pick up the packages they were purchasing with her credit card. She felt very insecure knowing there was someone out there with far more information than they should know, and the fact that her credit card company didn't believe her story only made it worse.

Keeli was overwhelmed by the feeling of having to "prove" who she was to someone who didn't even know her. To make a long story short, the situation was eventually resolved in her favor, but it brought up a lot of anxiety and insecurity in the meantime.

Doesn't this sound just like the enemy? He can cause so much confusion and distract you from your true identity, leaving you feeling like something is wrong with *you* at the end of the day when it is really *his* lies that have been assaulting your heart.

Have you ever felt the need to prove yourself to someone else? Why do you think you felt this way?

_____

_____

_____

_____

Even Jesus Himself had to deal with the lies of the enemy attacking His identity. Let's pick up the story in Matthew 4:

> *Then Jesus was led by the Spirit into the wilderness to be tempted by the devil. After fasting forty days and forty nights, he was hungry. The tempter came to him and said, "If you are the Son of God, tell these stones to become bread"* (Matthew 4:1-3).

> *Jesus answered, "It is written: 'Man shall not live on bread alone, but on every word that comes from the mouth of God'"* (v. 4).

Notice how the enemy challenged Jesus' identity by trying to make Him prove Himself. What I love most about how Jesus responded is that He quoted the Word of God (Deuteronomy 8:3, to be exact!). Jesus didn't need the "perfect words," because He had God's Word. You would think that would have done the trick, but the enemy fired back by attacking his identity yet again:

> *Then the devil took him to the holy city and had him stand on the highest point of the temple. "If you are the Son of God," he said, "throw yourself down. For it is written: "'He will command his angels concerning you, and they will lift you up in their hands, so that you will not strike your foot against a stone'"* (v. 5-6).

He must have thought he could outsmart Jesus by quoting Psalm 91 out of context, but Jesus was smarter than that, as He replied with a verse from Deuteronomy 6: *Jesus answered him, "It is also written: 'Do not put the Lord your God to the test'"* (v. 7).

Do you see the way that the enemy was undermining Jesus' identity? *If you are the Son of God …* The enemy was attempting to make Jesus doubt His true identity as the Son of God. He was trying to get Him to feel insecure and feel the need to go out of His way to prove who He was.

What makes this portion of Scripture so significant is what happened right before it:

> *As soon as Jesus was baptized, he went up out of the water. At that moment heaven was opening, and he saw the Spirit of God descending like a dove and alighting on him. And a voice from heaven said, "This is my Son, whom I love; with him I am well pleased"* (Matthew 3:16-17).

Hold up. Jesus had just heard the audible voice of God declare who He was—and not only who He was, but that the Father was pleased with Him—and then forty days later, we see the enemy whispering a blatant lie, essentially asking the Son of God, "Who do you think you are?!"

The enemy has a way of continually undermining your identity. He did this to the Son of God and continues to do this to God's daughters. But just as Jesus overcame the enemy's assault on His identity, you can overcome every attack on your identity through Christ who strengthens you!

I think the enemy realized he needed to switch up his strategy a bit when he tempted Jesus a third time. Realizing that Jesus was secure in His identity and felt no need to prove Himself, the enemy dropped the "who do you think you are" line and cut straight to the chase: *Again, the devil took him to a very high mountain and showed him all the kingdoms of the world and their splendor. "All this I will give you," he said, "if you will bow down and worship me"* (Matthew 4:8-9).

Seriously? The enemy was offering Jesus what was already His! I think Jesus was done with the lies at this point because of the way He responded next: *Jesus said to him, "Away from me, Satan! For it is written: 'Worship the Lord your God, and serve him only'"* (v. 10).

Want to know what happened next? *Then the devil left him, and angels came and attended him* (v. 11). Bye, Felicia!

In Scripture, the enemy is commonly called "the accuser" (Revelation 12:10). His attacks often come in the form of accusations that cause you to doubt who you are in Christ. He tries to convince you that you are not enough and that God is not enough to redeem any situation you may get yourself into. However, the Bible clearly tells us otherwise. You were created in God's image (Genesis 1:26), you have been redeemed by the blood of Jesus (Ephesians 1:7), and you have been invited to partake in God's divine nature (2 Peter 1:4). You were not an accident or a mistake (Psalm 139:16), you have a purpose (Jeremiah 29:11), you are deeply loved (Ephesians 2:4), your King has already won the ultimate victory (Colossians 2:15), and you have everything you need for this life (2 Peter 1:3). These are just a few of the Scriptures that reveal each of these truths; there are countless more throughout the Bible.

The truth of who God says you are is the only truth there is no matter how much "evidence" the enemy may present to try to convince you otherwise. *Look what you did—and you call yourself a daughter of the King. You're a terrible wife. You're a lousy mother. You're stupid. No one will ever love you. You don't fit in. Did you hear what they said about you?* IT'S ALL LIES! Every negative word spoken by you or against you is a lie.

I don't care how bad you blew it; there is nothing that is outside of God's power to redeem and restore. Sometimes, the enemy takes areas where we have legitimately messed up, heaps shame onto our heads, and drives us further away from God. Other times, he pulls things out of thin air that have absolutely no truth in them. It is time for us to expose the lies of the enemy and recover the truth of who God says we are.

In order to walk through this journey of discovering your true identity, you must first recognize the labels that have left a residue on your heart. You may not struggle with negative self-talk or "labeling" yourself. Even if you don't have any negative labels attached to you, have you allowed the label of your job title, the label of being a stay-at-home mom, or the label of being a wife, grandmother, or aunt be the thing that gives you value and a sense of worth? There are times when even the blessings in our lives become the things we look to in order to measure how successful or worthy of love we are.

Maybe you are like me and struggle with what others think of you. For most of my life, I proudly wore the label of "people-pleaser." I allowed this label to remain stuck to me despite God's attempts to rip it off on several occasions. I am not a big fan of learning the same lessons over and over, but it took me years to recognize that my own thoughts had created a "false self" that covered up who I truly was. I was becoming the words that would flash across my mind, and the labels were beginning to cause me to live for less than

I was created for.

At times, ripping off the labels that you have allowed to define you may be a quick and painless process, but there are other times when it will feel like ripping off a Band-Aid. When I was younger, I hated getting hurt, because I knew my mom would get the Band-Aids out which often hurt worse than the wound itself. I would throw a fit as my mom slapped a Band-Aid on my boo-boo, and she would try to get me to stop screaming by telling me there was "Jem and the Holograms" on it (if you don't know who Jem and the Holograms are, I am going to need you to Google that). In reality, these silly characters did nothing to mask the pain when it was time for the Band-Aid to be removed. It didn't seem to matter whether she pulled it off slowly or quickly; it was painful either way.

Removing your labels may hurt a bit, but healing comes right after the wound gets some fresh air. The words God speaks over you are the only words that matter, and I pray that His words are the breath of fresh air you need to rise up and receive your healing.

I pray that the Word of God cuts through the lies and shows you what is true. His Word is *alive* and will expose your true thoughts and desires. Remember, not everything that makes its way into your mind is truth; not every thought you have reflects what is true about you.

In order for us to embrace our true identity, we have to let go of the words that others have spoken about us or to us, and accept what the Word of God says about us.

TAKE A DEEP BREATH

I know what you may be thinking—who is this girl who referenced janky bangs and Jem and the Holograms?! In case you cannot yet tell, I love to laugh, and my Tennessee accent comes out from time to time. It's amazing that God has brought all of us together for this journey. There are women from nearly every state who participate in the Beautifully Designed Bible studies and will be reading this book, which absolutely amazes me. I am grateful for the opportunity to share how I overcame my identity crisis and discovered my true value in Christ so that I can, hopefully, help take you on the same journey.

As I have said previously, this book is designed to be more of an experience and a journey than just another book you read and put back on the shelf when you're finished. Discovering your identity in Christ is a lifelong process that won't happen simply by reading a book; however, this book may very well be the catalyst that God uses to start the process in your life.

My team and I have compiled the core Scriptures from this book so you can easily download them from our website, print them, cut them out, and place them around your home. You can put them on your bathroom mirror, in your kitchen or dining room, on your desk, in the car—any place where you need to be reminded of the truth on a daily basis.

Download these Scriptures at www.beautifullydesigned.com/PrintScriptures.

Dinner is a special time in the Shepherd home. As we eat, we each go around the table and share our high and low points of the day. Ryan and I take this time to encourage our boys and remind them that they are loved. Regardless of what is taking place in our lives, love is what all of us crave.

How would your life change if you realized how much you are loved?

....

....

....

Spend a few minutes in prayer asking God to reveal the depth of His love for you and erase every lie that has gotten in the way of you receiving that love.

....
....
....
....

MAKING THE EXCHANGE

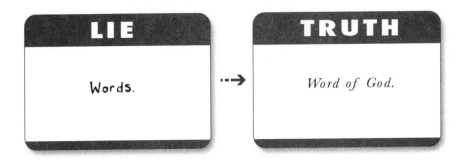

For the word of God is alive and powerful. It is sharper than the sharpest two-edged sword, cutting between soul and spirit, between joint and marrow. It exposes our innermost thoughts and desires.
~ Hebrews 4:12, NLT

Chapter 3

Self-Image

self-image
- [self-im-ij]

noun
1. the idea one has of one's abilities, appearance, and personality.

Before we dive into this chapter, I want you to put down this book and go look at yourself in the mirror. (I know you're probably comfortable, but just trust me.) Now, write down the first word that comes to mind when you see yourself:

Once you've done this, text one of your friends or family members and ask them to describe you in one word. (Go ahead, I'll wait until they text you back.) What was the word(s) they used to describe you?

Now, compare these words—are they similar or different? Do the words that others who know you align with the words you use to describe yourself? I'm willing to bet that the words of others are closer to aligning with the words that God speaks over your life. Why is it that we tend to only see our flaws when everyone else sees beauty?

I believe *every* woman struggles with self-image at some point in her life. Whether we want our curly hair to be straight or our waist to be a few inches smaller, we women never seem to be content with the way we look. I could tell you story after story of labeling myself as fat and ugly. For years, looking in the mirror felt like a punishment. Either my hair looked bad, my eyes looked weird, I was too flat-chested, or my butt was too big.

When was the first time you can remember feeling insecure about your appearance?

_____

_____

_____

Growing up in the 80s, it started with who had the best "jelly" shoes, then it became about who had the biggest hair. Don't even get me started on leggings. (Thank goodness those are back in style!) I'll never forget the first time I realized my clothes weren't "name brand." A girl in my class pointed it out, and when I looked down, I was reminded that they weren't even *my* clothes; I was wearing my sister's hand-me-downs!

You know that feeling when you realize you look different from everyone else? In those moments, most young girls either want to hide or make their mom take them on a shopping spree. In my family, neither was an option, leaving me with the urge to change the way I looked.

From that moment on, labels regarding my self-image began to attach themselves to me. It became like a game that I never wanted to play. I went back and forth from feeling like I needed to just blend in so no one would notice me to attempting to make it into the "cool kid" club—you know, that table of girls that wave you over when you walk into the school cafeteria. I became really good at dressing a certain way and playing the role of a cool kid at school in order to fit in, but when I would arrive home, I would change into my basketball clothes and go back to being Ashley. Looking back, I can see that this was when my people-pleasing first began.

Isn't it crazy how something so insignificant (in the grand scheme

Self-Image

of things) can attach itself to you and define the rest of your life? When I was in middle school, fitting in was all that mattered. Now that I'm an adult, married, and have two kids, it shouldn't matter whether or not people like me, but I often still find myself wearing that label and going out of my way to please people instead of just being myself.

Out of the labels you have identified so far, can you tell where they came from? Can you remember the moment you first felt that way? Ask God to show you when those labels first attached themselves to you and speak His truth over those areas of your life.

_____

_____

_____

_____

_____

I can also remember the girls at school laughing at me, because, in their opinion, my eyes were too big for my head. (Who even says that?!) I would stand in front of the mirror and practice talking without moving my eyes, so I wouldn't look weird when I talked to them the next day at school. I never felt like I was able to perfect the way my eyes moved as I talked, so the thought that I looked weird totally consumed me. My self-image was deteriorating based on what others thought of me which drove me to change the way God created me.

Being a preacher's kid, I was raised in a God-centered home. When I was young, I loved reading my Bible storybook and had a desire to spend time in the Word of God. However, as I grew older and my Bible was "upgraded," I began to feel intimidated. *What is up with all these names of different people in Leviticus?!* There were many seasons of my life when I would cherry-pick the "feel-good" verses from the Bible and not dive any deeper.

In a more recent season of my life, I thought it would be great to read the Bible from cover to cover, especially since I was now a mom and wanted to teach my boys to develop a love for God's Word. Unfortunately, I didn't get very far before I quit (which is an entirely new label we will discuss later), but I did come across one story I think most of us can relate to.

In Genesis 25, we begin following the story of Jacob. At one point, he is traveling and comes across "the people of the East" (Genesis 29:1). As he is chatting with these folks, a young girl named Rachel approaches, her father's sheep in tow. I'm sure you can guess what happens next. Smitten, Jacob runs to find Rachel's father and ends up staying in his home for a month, where he serves the family. Rachel's father, Laban, tells Jacob he will give him something in return for his service. Without missing a beat, Jacob tells Laban that he will work seven years for the right to marry Rachel. They both agree that this is a fair deal, so Jacob begins working.

It just so happens that Rachel has an older sister, Leah. While Rachel is beautiful in every way, Genesis 29:17 describes Leah as having "weak eyes." *(I know how you feel, Leah!)*

Seven years pass, and Laban gathers everyone in town for a wedding feast. But toward the end of the evening—you know, the part where the newly married couple go back to their hotel—Laban pulls a switcheroo. Instead of giving Jacob his younger daughter, Rachel, he gives him his older daughter, Leah!

Now it came to pass in the evening, that he took Leah his daughter and brought her to Jacob; and he went in to her. ... So it came to pass in the morning, that behold, it was Leah (Genesis 29:23, 25).

I am going to go out on a limb and say there must have been alcohol involved at this little feast. How else would you not realize you're with the wrong girl until the next morning?!

Needless to say, Jacob is a bit upset that he has been duped. He ends up confronting his father-in-law, who casually replies that it wouldn't be right for the younger daughter to marry before her older sister. Though he brings up this social custom, I think, in reality,

Self-Image

Laban thought that since Leah was older and wasn't pretty, the only way to get her married off would be to trick Jacob into marrying her.

My heart aches for Leah, as I can't help but wonder if she was constantly compared to her little sister. I seriously doubt she had a positive self-image, especially since her new husband didn't even want her! I can certainly relate to Leah's feelings of insecurity and rejection even though my story was obviously a bit different from hers (thank God!).

What you believe about yourself matters. The word you wrote down at the beginning of this chapter is a good indication of where you are at in terms of your self-image. One morning, I felt a lot like Leah as I looked in the mirror and immediately labeled myself as "fat."

It would be years before I would take this label off. I wore it every day; the number on the tag on my jeans defined how I felt about myself. Once I hit 280 pounds, it felt as though the label was permanently attached to me with no hope of it ever being removed. Every time I would go into my closet only to discover the clothes I wanted to wear were too tight, I would have a meltdown. I would sink to the floor of my closet as tears soaked the clothes I held in my hands. I would hear my husband yelling for me to hurry up, which only made things worse, because I knew there was no way he could possibly understand. He could eat seven donuts and have abs; I would get bigger just by smelling them. I began to resent that he could walk into his closet to pick out an outfit without thinking twice. Sunday was always the worst, because I could never find anything nice to wear that actually fit. My anxiety level would be through the roof as I walked into church with my family, hiding behind a fake smile so no one would see that I hated the way I looked.

One day, I felt God tugging on my heart. I knew something had to change. I honestly didn't know how I had become so consumed with anxiety over my hair, the wrinkles on my face, and the dimples on my legs. No wonder my self-image was so negative! I had given in to self-sabotage. My confidence and security was wrapped up in the number on the scale, and I was allowing that to define who I was.

Why do you think we tend to focus on the things we don't like about the way we look rather than the things we do like? Do you find yourself doing this?

_____

_____

_____

I was reading the Bible one day when I came across a verse I have read many times. This time, however, God spoke to me in a special way through this verse: *So God created mankind in his own image, in the image of God he created them; male and female he created them* (Genesis 1:27).

There have only been a few times I have felt like God was speaking to me "audibly," but on this particular day, I heard a gentle whisper to my heart that said, "Stop bashing Me. You are mine."

I looked around, unsure as to whether it was God speaking or just my own mind. It was then that I heard it again. "Stop bashing me. You are mine."

The voice wasn't "audible" in the sense that I heard it out loud as we would speak to one another, but that did not make it any less powerful. Tears began to well up in my eyes as I realized that the God of the universe actually *noticed* me—which excited and scared me at the same time.

All this time that I had been bashing myself for the way I looked, I was actually bashing God. He knew all my thoughts, words, and actions related to my physical appearance. The resulting negativity was beginning to spill over to every area of my life, and He intervened. Those words from God began to rip off the labels "fat" and "ugly" that I had placed on myself, as I accepted His invitation to see myself through His eyes.

Self-Image

This radically shifted the way I saw myself, and I have not been the same since. The journey, however, has not been without its share of ups and downs. Even as I was writing this book, there have been things that have taken place that have challenged my new self-image that came from looking at myself through God's eyes.

As summer approached, Ryan suggested we take the kids to the local public pool. In that moment, I wanted to run and hide as feelings of dread began to overtake me. Though I had a strong desire to make memories with my kids, the insecurity I felt at the thought of being seen in public in my bathing suit began to overwhelm me.

As I was sitting there, engaged in a mental tug-of-war, I heard my oldest say, "Mom never wears her bathing suit." My heart sank when I realized the last two times I had taken them to the pool, I had just watched them swim while I was fully clothed. I began to get upset as I realized how much my boys wanted their mom to swim with them, knowing that doing so would require letting go of my negative self-image and fear of what people would think of me. I pushed these thoughts aside, quickly changed into my bathing suit, pulled a cover-up on over it, and got in the car with my family.

On the drive over, I had to fight back tears as I thought of all the people who might see me at the pool, since I live in a small town. I slid my sunglasses on and tried to distract myself from thinking about this, but it continued to haunt me. As we pulled into the parking lot, my eyes scanned back and forth looking to see if there were any cars I recognized. When I saw a few, my heart sank.

As we entered the pool area, Wilson and Levi ran straight to the diving board. I had already made up my mind that I was keeping my cover-up on. I would still get some sun; I just wouldn't be in the water with my family. I found a spot to camp out and took video on my phone of the boys, cheering them on and offering ideas of different ways they could dive into the water.

As I began to look around the pool, I decided to let what God said about me become louder than my insecurities and fears. Standing up,

I removed my cover-up and began to make my way toward the diving board. Climbing the steps, I walked to the end of the board and leaped into the water. My dive was not perfect by any means, but it sure was freeing! In that moment, my identity was not wrapped up in how I looked in a bathing suit but was found in the One who beautifully designed me. Letting go of negative perceptions of my self-image brought a freedom that was indescribable. The laughter and smile of my boys as we splashed about the pool together was proof that I'd made the right choice.

Do you believe you were created in God's image?

_____

_____

How does this make you feel in light of your current perspective of your appearance?

_____

_____

_____

After the day that I took a leap of faith and dove into a pool, I began to feel a growing desire to dive deeper into the Word of God as well. I found it was filling a void I hadn't realized existed, and I was craving more.

A few weeks passed. I was getting ready one morning when one of my boys (who was just four years old at the time) came into my room and shouted, "Mom, I am having a fat day!" My heart immediately sank as I scooped him up in my arms, knowing he had heard that line from me. I explained to him that I would say that on days when I felt insecure which isn't how God created me to be. He just looked up at me, and I told him I was sorry for being so negative toward myself.

In that moment, I felt the Lord tug on my heart again. I felt that He was saying, "What if your children grow up speaking to themselves

Self-Image

the way you speak to yourself? Are you okay with that?" Absolutely not! My boys are champions, and I want them to be fully confident that they can do anything and become all God created them to be.

I then felt as though the Lord was scooping me up in His arms just as I had my son. He reminded me that He desires the same for me; He wants me to live confident in who He created me to be. And when I'm able to do this, it won't just impact my life; it will impact the lives of those I influence, beginning in my home. When I think back on that day, it still gives me chills.

I want you to stop what you're doing right now. Just be still and quiet. Set a timer for three minutes and close your eyes. Don't look at your phone. Don't think about the mess in the other room. Don't allow any distractions to take away from this time. Empty your mind of things that don't matter and be still for a moment, just you and God. Go ahead; I'll wait right here until you're done.

That felt awkward, didn't it? The first time I did this, I glanced at my phone after I thought it had been three minutes, only to find that just one minute and twenty seconds had passed. It was then that I realized I had filled my life with constant busyness and noise. I knew I needed to create new habits and become used to being still with God.

Those of us married women like myself often feel guilty when we aren't doing dishes, folding laundry, wiping noses, encouraging a friend, or taking care of our families. In the midst of the busyness, it can be difficult to hear the voice of God speaking to our hearts. He is always speaking, but we often have a hard time hearing His still, small voice through the noise of our lives. It is essential that we learn to embrace the silence and take time to just be still. These are the moments when our souls are recharged, as God reminds us that we are "fearfully and wonderfully made" (Psalm 139:14).

If you ever feel like you're not pretty enough, if you ever feel like you're too fat or too skinny, allow God to take you in His arms and fill your heart with confidence as He reminds you that you are beautifully designed. You may think you're not enough, but He sees you as more than enough. You may think you're plain and ordinary, but He sees you as lovely. Which voice is the loudest in your head?

TAKE A DEEP BREATH

Throughout this chapter, I have attempted to help you identify the moments where you allowed negative labels to define the way you see yourself. Now is the time for you to dive a bit deeper and ask yourself what truly matters—is it your own thoughts, the opinions of others, the lies of the enemy, or the voice of God?

There comes a time when you must ask yourself *why*. Why focus on your negative attributes? Why become consumed about what someone else thinks of you? Why give in to the lies of the enemy? Why do you not believe the truth of who God says you are? Why has negative self-talk become such a habit?

Write down any lies you have allowed to become attached to you regarding your physical appearance and self-image.

_____

_____

_____

It may be difficult to read the words you just wrote down. You may be thinking something along the lines of "I can't believe I actually had those thoughts about myself!" I don't know about you, but I want to live with the heart of a warrior, with a mindset that says, "Regardless of my waist size, how many wrinkles I have, or what my hair looks like, *I am beautiful!*"

I don't know what your background is. You may not have had parents like mine who connected you to Jesus and modeled what it looks like to live life with Him at the center. You may not have begun a relationship with Jesus yet, or you may have had one before, but over time, decided that you would take control of various pieces of your life and begin writing your own story.

Self-Image

Regardless of where you are at in your walk with the Lord, you can choose today to rise up and replace the negative thoughts related to your self-image with God's truth. You may think it's cheesy and a bunch of hocus pocus, or you may choose to take Jesus' hand and allow Him to show you how loved you truly are—in spite of your looks, thoughts, feelings, actions, or the opinions of others.

When you come to realize that the King of the universe beautifully designed you and that you are beautiful, regardless of your "imperfections," there is nothing that can convince you otherwise. This is why it is critical that you take time to slow down and listen to the One who knitted you together perfectly. When you do this, your identity will become rooted in Christ rather than in your physical appearance.

MAKING THE EXCHANGE

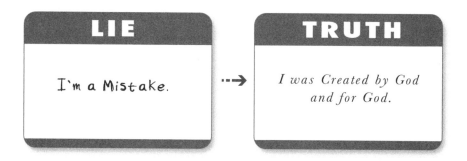

"Then God said, 'Let us make mankind in our image, in our likeness, so that they may rule over the fish in the sea and the birds in the sky, over the livestock and all the wild animals, and over all the creatures that move along the ground.' So God created mankind in his own image, in the image of God he created them; male and female he created them." ~ Genesis 1:26-27

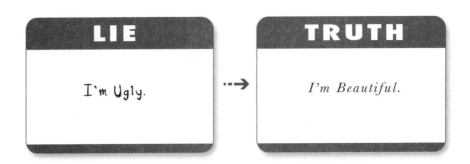

"I praise you because I am fearfully and wonderfully made; your works are wonderful, I know that full well." ~ Psalm 139:14

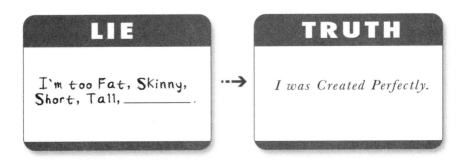

"For you created my inmost being; you knit me together in my mother's womb." ~ Psalm 139:13

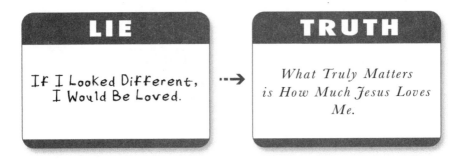

"This is how we know what love is: Jesus Christ laid down his life for us." ~ 1 John 3:16a

Chapter 4

Failure

failure
- [feyl-yer]

noun
1. Lack of success.
2. An unsuccessful person or thing.
3. A lack or deficiency of a desirable quality.

Failure is a label that so many of us wear. We live much of our lives terrified of failure and rejection, and these two fears go hand-in-hand. We fear not being successful, and we fear the rejection that will inevitably come when we are unsuccessful. The failure we fear doesn't always happen, but when it does, we are often left feeling like we are not enough. When this happens repeatedly without being addressed, our dreams begin to die, and we resign ourselves to just "getting by" in life, trying desperately to avoid the label of failure that seems to remain attached to us.

There have been many days when I have whispered the words "I am a failure" to myself, often many times throughout the course of the day before my head hits the pillow. The most recent time that this occurred is kind of a funny story.

Last week, I asked my assistant, Amber, to watch my boys while I went and got my hair done. Summer had just begun, and Ryan was on a two-week business trip, leaving me to run my business and care for Wilson, Levi, and our new puppy, Wrigley (the cutest goldendoodle ever). We were four days in, and I was confident that my scheduled hair appointment had been divinely orchestrated.

Amber brought her son, Reed, over to play with the boys, and I left to be pampered for a few hours. I turned out of my driveway and was about nine seconds down the road when I received a call that my five-year-old was having a meltdown over being asked to pick up his toys. Amber put Levi on the phone, and we had a nice chat which consisted of me threatening to take away baseball camp if he didn't pick up his toys. (Let's be real, this would have been more of a punishment for me than for him!)

After hanging up the phone, I let out a long sigh and told myself that in less than twenty minutes, a stylist would be massaging my head as I enjoyed two hours of relaxation and "girl talk" before heading back home to begin checking things off my to-do list.

A few hours later, the feeling of serenity immediately vanished as I walked through my front door. Amber quickly informed me that Wrigley had gotten ahold of rat poison. She was able to get it out of his mouth in time but suggested I call a vet to be safe. As I was dialing the number for the vet, we heard crying from the boys' room. Being a mother of boys for eight years now, I defaulted to my learned behavior and ignored it, thinking they would come find me if there was blood or any broken bones.

The next thing I knew, Reed was walking out of the room crying and holding his nose. Blood was everywhere. Wilson, my oldest, was a few steps behind, crying as well. "It was an accident!" he exclaimed through tears.

Between stopping the blood that was gushing from Reed's nose and trying to calm Wilson, who was hysterical because he thought he was in a lot of trouble, I noticed that Wrigley was acting weird. Of course, all of this took place while I was on the phone with the vet, who had not yet picked up the phone.

We got Reed fixed up, and my fears subsided as the vet assured me that Wrigley would be fine. As I hung up the phone, I walked across

Failure

the room to Wilson and asked him to explain what happened. We all talked for awhile, he apologized, and we went about our day. After Amber and Reed left, I secretly prayed that his nose wasn't broken and my dog wouldn't die. (I am so grateful this is not a parenting book! As you can see, I can barely hold it together some days, let alone offer sage wisdom on how to raise amazing kids that never get into trouble.)

I'm laughing now as I look back on that day, but it was terrifying at that moment. I felt like I had failed as a mom, all because I had taken a few hours for myself!

Those who are close to me know I have suffered with anxiety attacks in different seasons of my life. That evening, as my boys fell asleep and I quietly climbed into bed alone, my mind was swirling and my heart began to race. I had been on edge with the boys the rest of the day and was emotionally exhausted. I heard myself whisper, "I am a failure as a mom," aloud as tears began to roll down my cheeks.

It was then that my phone rang. Ryan was on the other end, asking how our day was. (If he only knew!) I informed him that everyone was still alive, though it was questionable what would happen to Wrigley, and told him I was about to fall asleep. I didn't tell him that I had been in tears moments before, as the word "failure" had placed itself across my heart. I simply tried to laugh it off and fall asleep before any other mistakes I had made earlier in the day could come to mind. I don't think I'll ever understand why it is so much easier to focus on my failures than all of the blessings in my life.

Do you struggle with the same habit of replaying the areas where you feel you failed at the end of the day? Are you harder on yourself than anyone else in your life? If so, why do you think you do this?

....

....

....

....

The word "failure" simply means "lack of success." When I attempt something and don't succeed, I'm often left feeling defeated and wearing the label "failure." This is a label I've found stuck to me many times in different seasons of my life, and if I was able to take a glimpse into your heart right now, I'm willing to bet I would find this label. The problem is, none of us succeed at everything all of the time. So why is it that we wind up wearing the label of "failure" when this is a normal part of life? Why is it that we focus on the things we "fail" at and often don't give ourselves enough credit for the things we had the courage to attempt and the areas where we excel?

If you were to succeed at nine things and fail at one, which would you find yourself focusing on? Would your one failure receive more than ten percent of your attention? Why do you think this is the case?

When was the last time you called yourself a failure?

What emotions were you feeling at the time?

The label "failure" can come when you make a mistake, quit something, or lose your temper. This is a big one for me. If I yell at my kids—even if they do things that cause me to experience strong and valid emotions—I often end up feeling like I have failed as a mom. In any area of my life where I am not perfect, I am vulnerable to feeling like a failure, and something tells me that I'm not the only woman who feels this way.

Some of you may find that you feel this way more often than

Failure

others. Some of you may only find yourself wearing this label when you really blow it; others of you will label yourselves as "failures" over small things like making a mistake at work, saying the wrong thing to someone, or cooking a meal for your family that didn't quite come out the way you envisioned it. Whether it's triggered by something large or small, this feeling does *not* represent what is most true about you, and it certainly doesn't represent the way God feels about you!

Ryan and I were married in 2005, and after returning from our honeymoon, I was excited to make our house a home and cook him his first meal. His mother is an amazing cook, so I wanted his first meal from his wife to really knock his socks off.

When he left for work that morning, the realization that I really didn't know how to cook began to settle in. I called my best friend, Donna Flynn, in a state of absolute panic. She responded by driving to my house and taking me to the grocery store. When we returned to the house, we quickly got to work. Donna walked me through the process of making mashed potatoes, green beans, and a chicken casserole. (Let's be honest, *she* made these things while I decorated the table; at least I could do that well!) After everything was prepped, Donna scooted out so it would look like I had cooked the meal myself. As she was leaving, she told me that I just needed to put the casserole in the oven for thirty minutes, and I'd be set.

I can totally handle this, I thought to myself after Donna left. I put the top on the casserole dish and followed her directions then jumped in the shower to freshen up before Ryan arrived home.

A few minutes later, I began to smell something terrible. I quickly got out of the shower and ran to the kitchen where I saw smoke coming out of the oven. In a panic, I opened the oven to see the *plastic* top of the dish melting into the casserole. *Oh no!* I thought. *I followed Donna's directions; she never said not to use the plastic top!* Looking back, I realize she probably thought this went without saying, but in the moment, I did not think twice about putting the plastic top of the casserole dish in the oven.

I immediately called Donna and was, fortunately, able to salvage *most* of the casserole. When Ryan got home an hour later, the smell of burnt plastic still lingered in the kitchen. So, I did what anyone would do and told him Donna had helped me cook the meal, and it was her fault. Just kidding! In reality, I told him the whole story, and he graciously ate "my" chicken casserole, which only had a little bit of a plastic taste to it.

Looking back, this is one of Ryan's and my best "newlywed stories," and Donna and I still laugh about it. But that night, my spirit was crushed. As I was getting ready for bed, I heard these words in my head: "You are such a failure. You can't even cook dinner for your husband. He is going to wish he had married someone else."

This label stuck to my heart for some time and created many insecurities that often left me feeling defeated. In reality, I had high expectations for how that night should have gone, and when the evening wasn't perfect, I felt like a failure. I was expecting too much of myself and putting pressure on myself to perform and to be perfect when that wasn't what Ryan expected from me at all. When I perceived that I was a failure, I allowed negative self-talk to become the dominant narrative in my mind and cloud out the blessings that were all around me.

I want to remind you of a Scripture I have already referenced. John 10:10 tells us we have an enemy who comes to steal, kill, and destroy. I believe the enemy wants women to feel defeated, so they shrink back in fear instead of rising up and stepping into all that God has for them. If he can cause us to focus on the negative things or what we perceive is wrong with our lives, he can cause us to miss what God is doing in our lives.

Earlier this year, I attended my son's school field day. Unfortunately, field day isn't the same as it was when I was younger. I'm competitive by nature, so I loved competing and obtaining as many ribbons as I could. I was really excited to see how many ribbons Wilson would win (he is fast!), but when I arrived, I was disappointed to see that they did not have ribbons at all. Instead, they had water

Failure

games, and most of them weren't even competitions. Water balloons and water guns? Emptying one bucket of water into another bucket? What kind of field day is that?!

They did, however, have one competition, a tug of war. As the field day came to a close, each class took their place on opposite ends of a thick rope. I could see the look of determination on the faces of the students as Wilson's class took hold of the rope. The other class looked fierce, but Wilson's class was ready to pull as hard as they could and knock the other kids down.

As the coach blew the whistle, a roar erupted from the crowd. (I may or may not have been a part of that.) The rope was being pulled back and forth aggressively, and I noticed that a few of the kids in Wilson's class let go, citing that their hands were hurting. This gave the other class the momentum they needed to win. I screamed for Wilson's class to pull hard, but as the words left my lips, it was the opposing class that responded with a hard tug on the rope. Wilson's class tumbled to the ground, and one kid burst into tears when his face hit the feet of the kid in front of him.

Wilson slumped over to where I stood, a look of defeat on his face. "Mom, I tried so hard," he said. Out loud, I reminded him that as long as he tried his best and had fun, it was a win. At the same time, however, I desperately wanted him to win a blue ribbon. (Are there any other competitive women out there who feel my pain?!)

This same tug of war is something most of us deal with on a regular basis, but it's not a tug of war with another class, your co-workers, or even your family; it's a tug of war in your heart. I feel this tug of war in my own heart—the desire to feel accomplished versus the pull of the label that says "I'm a failure" that can overwhelm me to the point where I just want to give up. I don't want to be one who let go because it hurts; I want those to be the moments when I pull harder and remain in the fight to the end.

Whether you realize it or not, we are all in a spiritual battle. This battle is much like a tug of war in our hearts; it's a battle to reject the labels the enemy puts on us to pull us down. It's a battle to believe the truth of what God says in the face of every lie. This is the time when we must not give up, when we must fight to create new habits of looking past our mistakes and failures and listening to the truth of who God says we are. Every day, we must choose to grab hold of the rope and fight for what we believe, and this will not be without resistance. Every day, you must choose to believe that God has a plan for your life, and you are not a failure—no matter how bad you've blown it!

I invite you to open your Bible and read Jeremiah 29:11. You can walk into Hobby Lobby and quickly find a beautiful wood sign that bears this Scripture. You can buy this sign and hang it in your house. You can see it on a cute social media graphic or even stitch it on a pillow and put it on your bed. But until you *believe* that this verse is true, it won't do you much good.

Go ahead, grab your Bible and read this verse. (If you don't have a Bible with you, you can look up this verse on your phone or the Internet.)

The truth that is found here can get watered down over time, especially since we quote this verse so often, and most of us who have grown up in church know it by heart. So, I want to take it a step further and do an exercise that will personalize this Scripture in your heart just as it was originally spoken to a specific group of people who God communicated with personally.

> Dear _____,
>
> I have so many plans for you! These plans are to prosper you so that you experience success as you walk through this life. My plans for you are not bad or evil, though bad things may have happened to you. I have a glorious future prepared for you. No matter what you experience in this life, and I want your heart to be filled with My hope.
>
> Love, Jesus

Failure

If you haven't already written your name on that blank line above, go ahead and do so right now. An important step in winning the battle to believe what God says about you is true is to actually believe that God's promises that you see in Scripture apply to *you*. There are times when we believe God's promises are true for others, but we don't believe they are true for *us*. For many of you, I think this is the first and most elaborate lie of the enemy that God wants to break so He can speak His truth to your heart.

If you go a bit further in Jeremiah 29, you'll see these verses: *Then you will call on me and come and pray to me, and I will listen to you. You will seek me and find me when you seek me with all your heart* (v. 12-13).

This is your "action step" for experiencing a good, successful, and hope-filled future—to seek after God with your whole heart and find His purpose for your life which starts with recognizing how loved you are and stepping into your true identity as God's daughter.

It's easy to wish we could wave a magic wand and get God to come and solve all our problems, but the reality is we need to be seeking Him with our whole hearts. When we do this, we will hear from God, who is more eager to speak to us than we are to ask Him to speak. When we reach out to the One who spoke the universe into existence, we will hear Him speaking to our own hearts.

God doesn't desire you to focus on the things you've failed at but to worship Him and to recognize that you are made in His image and have a purpose. Your identity is not based on whether or not you succeed at your job, have the best marriage, win "mother of the year," or retire with a million dollars in the bank. Your identity is found in Jesus Christ, and your purpose in this life is to grow in your relationship with Him as you step into your true identity and be a light in this dark world.

This life is not a dress rehearsal. There will never be another today; there will never be another "right now." Why would you spend an entire day that God has made lingering in a place of defeat and failure? Why would you stay down when you've been given everything you need to rise above? Why would you spend all of your time creating a façade of perfection when you've been set free to drop the pose and begin living a life of purpose?

If you're still feeling like a failure, I want you to grab a notebook and begin writing out a list of specific things you have accomplished and things God has blessed you with. Keep this list with you and don't allow a day to go by where you don't stop and thank Him for what you've already been given—regardless of what you may not have just yet.

If you ever feel your heart being tugged in the wrong direction, ask God to remind you of the things on this list. The Bible says the Holy Spirit will "teach us all things" and "bring all things to our remembrance" (John 14:26), so don't be afraid to ask Him to help you solidify these truths in your heart.

There is another word that is associated with failure and that word is *fear*. There are often times when many of us live with a fear of failure which can prevent us from attempting new things we should be able to courageously take on.

When I look back on the season of my life when I was full of insecurities and caught in a deep depression, I see how fear dictated the way I spoke and the decisions I made. I was tired of feeling like I was failing in my marriage, so I stopped putting effort into it completely and ended up listening to the lies that my marriage might fail. Ryan's flight schedule had him gone twenty-five consecutive days each month, which left me to raise our son alone (we just had one at the time). I had the thought that this might end up being how the rest of my life would look. My fears had me crying as I lay awake in bed each night; I felt like I was failing in so many different areas at the same time.

There wasn't one big issue in our marriage, but the distance between us and the loneliness we felt caused all of the little things to add up quickly. Ryan was a contract pilot, and he needed to be on every single flight in order to make enough money to pay our bills.

Failure

Since I never made enough money to pay for day care, we decided that I should stay home with Wilson, and we would get by on Ryan's income.

It was a difficult situation to be in. Though I was grateful to be home and appreciated Ryan's sacrifice for his family, I secretly resented him for missing out on every family memory. Every time he crawled into the cockpit of another airplane, more distance was created between us. There were many times when I thought to myself, *This is not what I signed up for.* I would cling to Wilson as I rocked him to sleep, silently praying that one day my husband would be home long enough to notice me.

Whether it is in your marriage, parenting, other relationships, or in your job, fear can creep in and cause you to feel like a failure, to the point that you might ask yourself, "Why am I even trying?"

Let's be honest. There are times when it is so much easier to quit. In those moments, we must allow God to come in and become bigger than our circumstances. When we do this, He will help us face our giants and give us the strength we need to believe the truth of who He says we are in the face of every lie.

There is a powerful story in the Old Testament that I believe will help us begin to peel off that label of "failure" once and for all. In Judges 6, we are introduced to a man named Gideon, a mighty warrior who has been called by God for a specific purpose. God sent an angel to tell Gideon that He was with him (v. 12). Gideon needed this reminder, because he was about to face a battle where the odds were against him, and the prospect of victory seemed bleak even though he had assembled an army of 32,000 men who were on his side.

Have you ever felt this way? Have you ever felt like you were facing a battle where the odds were stacked against you and failure was inevitable? These are the moments when you need to be reminded that God is near, so you can keep moving forward even when you're afraid that you might fail.

> *The Lord said to Gideon, "You have too many men. I cannot deliver Midian into their hands, or Israel would boast against me, 'My own strength has saved me.' Now announce to the army, 'Anyone who trembles with fear may turn back and leave Mount Gilead.'" So twenty-two thousand men left, while ten thousand remained* (Judges 7:2-3).

I have heard this story many times and have always wondered what it was that caused two-thirds of Gideon's army to turn back in fear. Perhaps it was a fear of the unknown, or maybe it was a fear of failure? I know I have dealt with both of these types of fear in my own life.

As we continue to follow Gideon's story, we see that the Lord told him to eliminate more men from his core army. This must have made absolutely *no sense* to Gideon. I can imagine him saying something like, "But Lord, I need these men to win!"

But God had a different plan. He whittled Gideon's army from 32,000 men down to 300 and then sent him off to battle. From an outside perspective, Gideon's army would surely fail. They had been outnumbered at 32,000, long before they were cut down to 10,000 and then 300.

In the end, Gideon's army didn't just win the battle; they sent the enemy running in fear! This certainly wasn't because Gideon was strong enough or prepared for the battle; it was because he was obedient to God in spite of the obstacles and instructions that would have seemed insane to the leader of any army. It's clear to me that God wanted Gideon and the people of Israel to understand that *they* were not the source of their victory; it was the power of God working through them, and He alone would receive the glory.

Do you ever feel like you are facing a battle and have no one to support you or the tools you need to overcome? When failure seems imminent, when you're not prepared for the fight, when you're feeling insecure and not sure how you will win the battle; in those moments,

Failure

it's important to remember that God is on your side, and He is all you need! You only need one weapon, and that is the Word of God.

Do you ever feel like you have failed in your relationships with those closest to you? If so, ask God what He wants to say about this.

Do you believe that God can restore failed relationships? (This doesn't necessarily have to be a spouse but could be family or close friends who you have become estranged from.)

As the weeks that Ryan and I were apart started to turn into months, I felt alone, and I wondered if I would be alone forever. I felt like Gideon when God was whittling down his army. When I listened to the lies of the enemy, the failure of my marriage seemed imminent. I remember many tear-filled nights when I asked God to take control and help me to fight for my marriage, but with the odds against us, I wasn't sure how we would overcome. There were nights when I would cry so loudly that I would have to cover my mouth, so my son wouldn't hear from the other room.

Looking back, I see how the enemy tried to isolate me and cause me to believe that I was the only one experiencing such deep hurt. During this time, I counteracted the enemy's lies by crying out to God like I never had before.

During this season, a friend randomly gave us a copy of the movie *Fireproof*. "It's such a great movie!" I remember her telling me. "My husband and I loved it."

Ryan and I decided to watch it together one night, and I'm pretty sure we cried through the entire movie. The couple in Fireproof had many of the same struggles and feelings of distance in their marriage; yet God restored them. Even though this was a fictional story, it gave us a glimmer of hope that God could restore our marriage as well.

A few weeks later, we heard that Kirk Cameron (who played the lead role of the husband in Fireproof) was coming to town, and Ryan and I knew we had to go hear him speak. We walked into a church near our home one night, feeling much like the "trembling warriors" who left Gideon when he told them they could turn back. But by the end of the night, God had filled our hearts with hope, and we realized that He would be with us. We recognized that the enemy was trying to divide us and made the decision that we would never quit fighting for our marriage. We knew this would be a difficult journey, but we also knew that we could lean on God for strength in those moments.

There were many days that followed when this decision was challenged. There were days when I felt like it was a losing battle and just didn't feel like continuing to fight. I couldn't fix Ryan being away so much, but I had hope that God would mend my heart and remove the bitterness I had allowed to creep in. I had to learn to lean on God's promise that He would never leave me or forsake me even when I felt my husband had "left" me for his job. Leaning on God's promise meant that I had to stop living my life based on my emotions and had to learn to crave God's presence over Ryan's during this season.

In the weeks and months that followed, Ryan and I rose above our circumstances and clung to God's Word, knowing that He was fighting for us and would lead, guide, and direct us. Soon, the enemies that stood in the way of our marriage began to flee, just like they did for Gideon's army, as we began to see that God was the true source of our strength.

TAKE A DEEP BREATH

It can be hard for women to open up and admit they are having issues. We don't want to admit we are struggling in our marriage, as parents,

Failure

in our work, or in any of our other relationships, because we don't want others to view us as failures.

This being the case, I'll go first: I don't have a picture-perfect marriage, I'm not the best cook, and I don't always make the best decisions when raising my boys. I've allowed the fear of failure to stop me from writing a book for at least ten years, and my life isn't always as awesome as it may appear on social media. There are days when the dishes don't get washed, the boys are dirty, and our house looks like *Toys R Us* threw up all over the place.

All of this overwhelms me, but I know that I can't allow it to make me feel like a failure. Because the truth is, I have a great marriage that has weathered many storms, I'm becoming a better cook (I think), and I'm learning how to be a better parent every day. I'm finally taking the steps to finish this book, and I'm grateful to be surrounded by an online community of women who I can be real and authentic with. My house may not always be clean, but let's be honest, is that really the most important thing in life? It's certainly not worth feeling defeated about!

I share these stories, because I believe that being transparent about our weaknesses and struggles gives us the opportunity to encourage one another. It is my hope that my story will set your heart free from the feeling that you have to be perfect, that you have to "measure up," that you can never fail. I want you to begin to see every part of your story as beautiful and to realize that you have been called by name by the Creator of the universe who did not design you to just "get by" in life.

There is no such thing as a "perfect" life, so you might as well stop striving to create one. Look around in the midst of the chaos, and ask God to help you to see it as beautiful even though it may be a bit messy at times. The mess doesn't make you a failure, because you have been called by God for a purpose, and your purpose is not to live a perfect life, but to be loved by God, discover your true identity in Him, and bring Him glory in the earth.

Can you identify where the label "failure" is trying to stick in your life?

....

....

....

....

Once you have identified where this label is affecting you, you'll be ready to face it head on. You don't need advice from 32,000 people or even 300; you just need to be reminded that God is near, and you can trust Him. Your successes or failures do not define who you are; only God can define who you are, and He has already declared that you are chosen (Ephesians 1:4-5), accepted (Romans 15:7), worthy (Psalm 8:4-6), and deeply loved (1 John 3:1). At the end of the day, you must choose to rest your identity in God not how clean your house is, how perfect your family is, or how successful you are at your job.

MAKING THE EXCHANGE

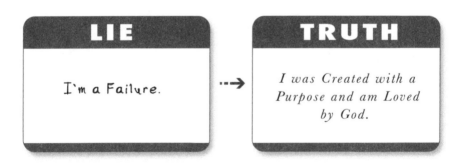

"For I know the plans I have for you," declares the Lord, "plans to prosper you and not to harm you, plans to give you a hope and a future." ~ Jeremiah 29:11

"See what great love the Father has lavished on us, that we should be called children of God! And that is what we are!" ~ 1 John 3:1

Failure

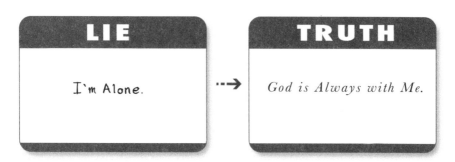

"For I am the Lord your God who takes hold of your right hand and says to you, Do not fear; I will help you." ~ Isaiah 41:13

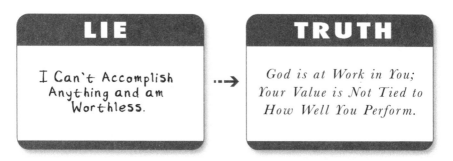

"...being confident of this very thing, that He who has begun a good work in you will complete it until the day of Jesus Christ." ~ Philippians 1:6

Chapter 5

Shame

shame
- [sheym]

noun
1. A painful feeling of humiliation or distress caused by the consciousness of wrong or foolish behavior.
2. A person, action, or situation that brings a loss of respect or honor.
3. A regrettable or unfortunate situation or action.

As I have been writing this book, I can see stay-at-home moms, working moms, single moms, high school students, college students, grandmothers, and great-grandmothers reading it as they seek to discover their identity in Christ, which is the core focus of this book and my ministry, Beautifully Designed.

I see *you* whether you're on your lunch break at work, curled up under a blanket in your favorite corner of the house, outside at a park, on vacation, sitting in bed, or on a bus, train, or plane. Regardless of what is on your plate right now, I just want you to know that I see you. You are seen, known, and loved—by God and by me, and you are the reason why I am writing this book.

I see women from all over the world, from all walks of life, craving a connection with something greater than themselves, seeking to be a part of a story larger than themselves, women who are exhausted looking for rest and peace, women who have been hurt and wounded by the battle of this life but are trudging on, sometimes barely keeping their heads above water.

As we have talked about the power of words, self-image, and failure, there has been an underlying question that is interwoven around all of these topics. That question is simply, "Where do you find your value?"

We sometimes find our value in our performance, the opinions of others, the way we look, the stuff we possess, our spouse and kids, or our titles and positions. However, I have come to realize that our true value can only be found in Jesus Christ, and He alone has the power to define and label us.

When we turn to other things to tell us we are valuable, we often find that we do not measure up. That's where feeling like a failure can come in. If my value is in how awesome my kids are, what will happen to me when my kids do something that isn't awesome? What happens if they don't turn out the way I thought they would? What happens when they, inevitably, move out of the house and begin to separate their lives from mine?

If my value is found in my title or position, what happens if my season of life changes and I end up staying home to raise my kids? What happens if I lose my job? What happens if my position changes, or I don't receive the amount of praise I'm used to?

When our value is rooted in something other than Christ, it can easily be changed or threatened. If we lose the thing we looked to for our sense of value and purpose, it can cause us to experience a deeper feeling called *shame*.

The dictionary tells us that shame comes in when we are aware that we have done something wrong or foolish, when we lose our sense of respect or honor, or when we end up in an unfortunate situation.

However, I have found that these things can only cause a lingering sense of shame if we have placed our value in something other than Christ. For example, if my value is found in what people think of me, and my kids misbehave in public, I am going to feel a sense of

Shame

shame. But if my value is found in Christ, I am able to move forward with my life in spite of the shame, because I know that this does not define who I am.

I've got news for you—kids misbehave! Yes, I know that was very profound, but I think all mothers need to understand that their kids will not always be perfect, and this does *not* automatically mean you have failed as a mom.

This is why it is so important that our identity is rooted in Christ, because when it is, nothing in this life can shake us. However, when we place our identity and worth in fragile things, it will always be undermined, and we will be left feeling unworthy.

This is how shame works, but you have the power to overcome shame through the power of the cross! Jesus experienced a humiliating and shameful death to set you free from any feelings of shame that other people or this world try to put on you.

The book of Hebrews in the Bible tells us more about this:

> *Therefore, since we are surrounded by such a great cloud of witnesses, let us throw off everything that hinders and the sin that so easily entangles. And let us run with perseverance the race marked out for us, fixing our eyes on Jesus, the pioneer and perfecter of faith. For the joy set before him he endured the cross, scorning its shame, and sat down at the right hand of the throne of God* (Hebrews 12:1-2).

Have you ever looked for your sense of value and purpose in something external like a job or position?

....
....
....

If I were your enemy, I would do everything in my power to make sure your past mistakes haunt you. I would cause things out of your control to define you. I would convince you that you don't have a purpose, because you have a past. Guess what?? You *do* have an enemy that seeks to destroy your identity and remind you of your past mistakes!

I want to jump right into peeling off this label, because I know so many of us deal with it. You can't be alive for long without experiencing something that caused you to feel shame. In some of those moments, you did actually need correction for your disobedience, but the shame that followed seemed to linger long after the lesson was learned.

In my own life, much of my shame came from my own disobedience and sin. I think many of us have an internal struggle at times to be obedient even when we know it's what is best for us. I see this often with my boys!

One Sunday after church, we were feeding the boys ham sandwiches when our youngest, Levi, refused to eat. Ryan took Wilson outside to play while I told Levi he had to sit at the table and finish his lunch before he could join his dad and brother outside. Crying ensued, which gave way to anger, but I was prepared to stand my ground.

I've heard many older women who have raised their kids tell young mothers like myself that we will eventually learn to pick our battles. I'll tell you what, this was one that I was prepared to fight and win.

Levi stared at me for a solid five minutes without moving. I responded by looking at him and saying, "It's okay; I have *all* day to wait for you to finish your lunch!"

After the first half hour, I went to the laundry room to unload the washer when I heard Levi yell, "I'm done; I'm going outside!"

I walked back into the kitchen, saw his empty plate, and thought to myself, *that's right; I won!* (If you'll recall, I am very competitive.) I left the room again to finish the laundry then returned to clean up the kitchen. It was then that I noticed two pieces of ham at the top of the trash can.

It didn't take long for me to return to battle mode. I grabbed that ham, put it on a plate, called Levi back inside, and told him he had to eat it. I could see the struggle written across his face. Would he be obedient, or would he insist on doing what he wanted? It was the ultimate mommy/son stand-off. If you've raised or are currently raising kids, I'm sure you know what this is like.

Levi had just turned three and was one of the sharpest three-year-olds I had ever met. His trickery was creative, but in the end, mommy won, as Levi ate the ham that I had picked out of the trash.

Remember, this is not a parenting book! I do not necessarily recommend this strategy; some may think it is overly harsh or gross, but there are times when you have to teach your kids a lesson they will never forget.

The reason why I share this story is because it illustrates the concept of sin which each of us are born into. It all goes back to the beginning of the story, to the first humans to walk this earth. Adam and Eve were created by God, in His image, and placed in a beautiful garden where life was perfect, and they had everything they needed at their fingertips. They had unbroken connection with one another, and God was right there with them; it never felt like He was a million miles away. I love the idea that they were able to approach God directly and ask Him anything at any time.

However, God did not want His children to be robots; He didn't want to force them to love Him. So, He gave them another option. God told Adam and Eve they could eat freely from all the trees of the garden with the exception of *one* tree. This tree was called the tree of "the knowledge of good and evil" (Genesis 2:16-17).

This wasn't just about God telling Adam and Eve not to do something. It was actually Him giving them the option to walk away from Him and attempt to do life on their own, to rely on their own definition of what is right and what is wrong instead of following God and being obedient to Him. Think of it like a parent who knows what is best for their child, but the child insists on having their own way instead of listening to their parent's loving guidance.

The enemy than came to Eve in the form of a serpent and began to attack her with lies. He didn't try to convince her to go ahead and eat from the tree, he didn't give her a list of ten reasons why she should, and he didn't sit with her for hours describing how delicious the fruit would be if she ate it. Instead, he asked a simple question that undermined the voice of God: *"Did God really say, 'you must not eat from any tree in the garden?'"* (Genesis 3:1b).

What is important to realize is this was a total lie! God did NOT say they couldn't eat from *all* of the trees; He only told them not to eat from *one* tree! The enemy was doing the same thing he continues to do today—making up lies that cause us to doubt God's truth.

> *The woman said to the serpent, "We may eat fruit from the trees in the garden, but God did say, 'You must not eat fruit from the tree that is in the middle of the garden, and you must not touch it, or you will die'"* (v. 2-3).

I'm kind of proud of Eve, because she responded by quoting what God had said, except she did add an extra line. God did tell her not to *eat* the fruit, but He never told her not to *touch* it; she added that portion. When we add to what God has said to us, it sets us up for the enemy to come in and distort the truth with his lies.

> *"You will not certainly die," the serpent said to the woman. "For God knows that when you eat from it your eyes will be opened, and you will be like God, knowing good and evil"* (v. 4-5).

I have found that the enemy sometimes likes to mix little bits of truth with his lies in order to convince us to believe them. For example, one of the ways he can do this to women is by convincing us that we're fat. The "truth" may be that we are not as thin as we used to be, but when we start to believe his lie and say to ourselves things along the lines of *I could stand to lose a few pounds; maybe then I would be beautiful, and people would love me*, we fall right into the enemy's trap, as we have now allowed shame to take hold and convince us that our self-worth is tied solely to our outward appearance.

The portion of Genesis 3:4-5 that is partially true is where the enemy says "your eyes will be opened." The truth was Adam and Eve were *already* like God; they were already created in His image and likeness (Genesis 1:27). They didn't need to believe the lie of the enemy and reach for something to validate them, because they already possessed the very thing the enemy was tempting them to disobey God to obtain.

After Eve decided to give in to the lies of the enemy and disobey God by eating the fruit, she gave some to Adam as well (because who likes to sin alone!). Here's what happened next:

Then the eyes of both of them were opened, and they realized they were naked; so they sewed fig leaves together and made coverings for themselves (v. 7).

The enemy was right when he said their eyes would be opened, but he lied about what this would result in. He tried to convince them that they would obtain something they already possessed if they sinned, but, in reality, this sin brought about shame. Their eyes were opened, shame entered the human story, and they covered themselves, because they felt exposed (this isn't just about wearing clothes).

Because of this original sin, we are all born into sin today. We are naturally selfish, and we all struggle with the internal war of whether or not we will obey. We are born into this world where we all sin, and we all suffer from the sins of one another. This makes it impossible for any of us to have a perfect life; yet we often struggle to build perfect lives anyway. On top of all this, sin brings about shame, so when we can't obtain the elusive "perfect" life, we often begin to feel that there is something foundationally wrong with *us*. Shame doesn't look at sin and say, "I made a mistake." Instead, shame says, "I am a mistake."

In my own life, there have been many times when I have truly believed that there was something wrong with my personality—something wrong with *me*. I compare myself to others constantly, and I love to win so much that I tend to take shortcuts when I know I shouldn't. At the same time, I can be lazy and would rather chill on the couch all day when there are others things I should be doing. I'd probably be eating Oreos while on the couch, and I often feel the urge to hide rather than stepping into the things God has called me to.

If I'm honest, this chapter has been one of the hardest for me to write. Since I am naturally such a competitive person (okay, maybe I should just say "stubborn"), it can be difficult to admit when I make a mistake or disobey God. Additionally, I often find the label of "people-pleaser" sticking to my heart, and I can be overwhelmed thinking about how my actions let someone else down. And even though I have a strong desire to please people, I find myself doing things to let down the ones I care about the most time and time again.

Thankfully, I married a man who is naturally self-motivated which has balanced all of this out in a way that only God could orchestrate. I'm also reminded that I'm not the only one who struggles. Romans 3:23 says, *For all have sinned and fall short of the glory of God.* The word I want to focus on in particular is "all"—which in Greek means ALL. I'll be honest, it's comforting to know that I'm not the only one who messes up, especially when we live in a society where we tend to only show our best sides to the world. It's strangely comforting to know that every person who has ever lived has wrestled with the same temptations and sins that I have.

Well, now that you know that none of us are perfect (no matter how good our lives may look from the outside), and we are all in need of a Savior, let's talk about how the mistakes we've made have affected our lives and caused us to live in shame.

Have you ever kept your failures hidden, because you thought that others around you were "perfect" and wouldn't be able to relate?

Shame

How would your life change if you felt the freedom to be more honest about your shortcomings?

Regardless of where you have been or what you have done up to this point, the sins you may be entangled in right now, or where you will fall short in the future, we have a Savior who rescues us and is gracious toward us. Remember, it is the enemy (who you may now envision as a gross snake) who heaps shame on you and tries to make your past affect your present and even your future. He slithers around like a snake in the grass, and the New Testament uses the imagery of a different animal to describe him: *Stay alert! Watch out for your great enemy, the devil. He prowls around like a roaring lion, looking for someone to devour* (1 Peter 5:8, NLT).

This is interesting, because a lion in Scripture is most often used to describe Jesus as the Lion of Judah. That devil really is a snake, because he mixes little bits of truth with his lies and can sometimes cause us to believe that even God is disappointed in us when, in fact, the opposite is true.

I will never forget the day my friend and I decided to start an online Bible study, in the fall of 2015. Within four weeks, there were over 9,000 women on the Facebook page, and I almost had a heart attack. *God, I didn't sign up for this!* I recall thinking. *I'm not equipped to lead this many women.* At the same time, all of my past mistakes and current issues began to flood my heart. At the time, I had allowed the pressures and responsibilities of life to keep me from reading my Bible every day—and I was certainly no theologian. My husband and I were fighting, and I felt completely unqualified to lead a bunch of people; I just wanted to go deeper in God's Word with a few friends!

As I sat staring at a screen full of women, my anxiety levels began to rise. I imagined they were expecting a godly woman who knows all about the Bible to appear. *That's just not me*, I thought as I froze for a moment, searching for a way out. *These women don't want a woman who is struggling with anxiety attacks and fighting with her husband to lead them anyway. They deserve someone like Beth Moore, someone who has it all together, and can lead a professional Bible study.*

Shame began to rear its ugly serpent head, and I knew I had a choice to make. I knew I had to be obedient to God and move forward. This overwhelmed me, but I did it anyway; I stepped past my fears and led the Bible study even though I didn't "feel" like doing it. There are times when we have to rise up and refuse to allow our emotions to dictate our actions, and this was one of those times.

Some of the fears I faced—and even face now while writing this book—have to do with people not liking me or liking how I teach. I wrestle with whether or not I am sharing too little or too much of my story, and I wonder if I am accurately sharing the message that God has put on my heart to encourage others.

The enemy would love for me to focus on my anxiety, relational issues, and stand-offs with my children to the point where I close my computer and stop writing this book. He wants those issues to define me and cause me to doubt whether I'm really qualified to share this message of hope that the Lord has caused me to share with you.

I am the woman who has to slowly breathe in and out when she's in a large crowd, a woman who has to convince herself through tears to put on a bathing suit and take her kids to the pool, a woman who fears that her husband will leave her for someone smaller, prettier, and more driven. This is *real* life, and the reason why I am sharing these things is to let you in on a little secret—we *all* struggle. We just aren't all brave enough to say it out loud. (And I'm not even sure I'm brave enough, but I'm doing it anyway!)

Our struggles don't all look the same. Some have deeper levels of hurt involved, some are external struggles that are out of our control. Regardless of what our struggles may be, we need to realize that we are all in the same fight together, so there's no need to feel threatened by one another and try to compete with one another in unhealthy ways that tear us apart. That is exactly what the enemy wants! He seeks to "divide and conquer," because he knows if he can isolate us, it will be easier to defeat us.

> *Two are better than one, because they have a good return for their labor: If either of them falls down, one can help the other up. But pity anyone who falls and has no one to help them up* (Ecclesiastes 4:9-10).

Have your sin and failures left your heart overwhelmed with a sense of shame? How does this make you feel?

_____
_____
_____
_____

Do you trust God with your life? If so, write your name on the lines below.

I, _____, choose to accept God's grace over my life. I, _____, choose not to listen to the lies of the enemy but to live in the love of Christ and allow His Word to be the only thing that defines who I am.

Sometimes, it can be helpful to make a declaration and journal our commitment to Christ. If you feel like this would be beneficial to you, I invite you to journal further outside of this book.

I was listening to sermons from Graham Cooke one night, because I heard he had some great thoughts on identity in Christ. I came across one in particular that is featured on the Jonathan David & Melissa Helser album, *The Awakening*. I pressed play, unaware that this seven-minute message would change my life. Being a preacher's kid, I had heard about God's grace in at least 7,876 different sermons, but this one was different. As I sat in my office in the middle of the night, God began to peel away the shame label and replace it with His love.

The name of this short message is *Inheritance*, and you can find it on YouTube or Spotify. Be sure that you are in a quiet place where you can sit and listen with no distractions. I'll wait right here. I promise you that it is worth it. (If you come across the nine-minute version, Graham Cooke doesn't begin talking right away, so you'll hear worship music for the first minute or so.)

"He loves you, because He loves you; because He loves you; because He loves you; because He loves you …" How does this make you feel? Can you feel God's presence around you right now?

You, my friend, are so deeply loved. You are seen. You are known. You have a Savior who isn't concerned about your past sins, your current mistakes, or your insecurities; He simply loves and cares for *you*!

As Jesus carried His cross up to the top of a hill where he would die, He suffered greatly. When He reached the top, He was bloody and beaten, and He was nailed to that cross as blood dripped down onto the ground, covering more than just the dirt but the sin and shame of humanity.

When Jesus lifted His head and muttered his final words, "It is finished," your sin and shame were taken away. Three days later, He arose in victory which gives us hope that we, too, can rise and become new. When we are awakened to life in Christ, we can proclaim that we belong to Jesus, and His life is ours, because He lives! We can rise each morning with purpose, because a great price was paid for our redemption.

He loves you, because He loves you; because He loves you. Can you feel His love? Can you feel His arms wrapped around you, holding you? There is nothing you can ever do or not do that will make Him love you more than He does at this very moment. If you sense His love, go ahead and tell the enemy to get out of your head! You know where your true identity rests, and it's not in the lies the enemy throws at you in an attempt to keep you from coming to God and receiving His love.

Shame

The Scriptures tell us that the name of Jesus is the most powerful name that has ever existed (Philippians 2:9). Invite Him to take first place in your life, and declare the name of Jesus over your life, your spouse, your children, and in every room of your home. The enemy flees at the name of Jesus, leaving you free to choose grace over shame. And when shame tries to re-appear, you know where to take that label—the foot of the cross.

I want to share a story from the Bible that God has used in my life to remind me of His gracious love. In John 8, Jesus was ministering at the temple early one morning when a group of men came to him all upset. They were dragging a woman with them who was barely clothed, and they made her stand at the front of the crowd.

> *"Teacher, this woman was caught in the act of adultery. In the Law Moses commanded us to stone such women. Now what do you say?"* (John 8:4-5).

These men weren't concerned about the Law of Moses, they were trying to trap Jesus. They were trying to catch him off guard, and this woman was just a pawn in their sick little game. I can't even begin to imagine how she must have felt. Everyone was staring at her, condemning her, going as far as to say she should *die*! They didn't care to know her story; they just wanted to punish her for her actions.

This woman had a past, but she did not know if she would have a future. In this present moment, she stood before the crowd and before Jesus, hanging her head. I imagine tears filled her eyes and shame filled her heart, knowing that she was about to be beaten to death with rocks because of her sin. That was what happened to those caught in adultery back in the day, but that was before Jesus stepped into the story.

Fortunately, Jesus was smarter than these men that were hassling Him. He knew they were trying to trap Him, and He didn't feel pressured to respond to their demands to offer His opinion. Instead, He bent down and began writing in the dirt with His finger. We don't know what He wrote, but it must not have been enough for them at first, because they continued to question Him (v. 7a). Jesus then stood up, looked them in the eyes, and said, *"Let any one of you who is without sin be the first to throw a stone at her"* (v. 7b).

I am sure they were shocked, because Jesus shifted their attention from the woman to their own hearts. They were probably confused at first, but then the reality set in that Jesus was saying this was not their time to pretend to be judges. Jesus stooped down and began writing in the dirt again, and the men began to walk away. The oldest ones left first, then the younger ones (because those of us who have lived longer know you can't outsmart Jesus!), until Jesus and the woman were the only ones left.

> *Jesus straightened up and asked her, "Woman, where are they? Has no one condemned you?"*
>
> *"No one, sir," she said.*
>
> *"Then neither do I condemn you,"* Jesus declared. *"Go now and leave your life of sin"* (v. 10-11).

In that moment, Jesus covered her shame with His love and grace. He *declared*, "I do not condemn you," giving her hope and a future (literally). He set her free from her old life into her destiny. He gave her permission to live differently, to leave all she had ever known behind and walk into a new life of freedom.

Once Jesus sets us free, we have to stand and fight against the enemy who will try to pull us back into our old lifestyles and ways of thinking. When we mess up, the enemy will hit us with shame and convince us that Jesus won't take us back, so we might as well give in and return to our old ways. This is a lie! We will make mistakes; we will not live *perfect* lives after we walk away from our sin and shame, but in those moments when we do stumble and fall, we will get back up and cling to Jesus, refusing to allow the enemy to get inside our heads and heap shame upon us to make us feel unworthy like the men tried to do with the woman in the story.

TAKE A DEEP BREATH

Walking out of your shame can be difficult, especially if you've lived in the darkness for so long. Removing this label might feel like ripping off a Band-Aid, but I promise you it is worth it. When you allow God's love and grace to replace this label, you will be able to walk in freedom.

In what areas of your life do you feel lingering shame?

_____
_____
_____

Can you identify where that shame entered and became a part of your story?

_____
_____
_____

What would it look like if you let go of your shame and began to re-write your story with God?

_____
_____
_____

My prayer is that you will be able to see God removing all shame from your past, present, and future, and you will grow in your relationship with Christ in order to be continually reminded of how loved you are.

He loves you, because He loves you; because He loves you, and there is nothing you can do or not do that will make Him love you any less!

If this is the first time you have read about how Jesus died for you and is alive today, I want to encourage you to reach out to a friend or someone at a local church near you. If you would like to contact our ministry team, you may to do at beautifullydesigned.com/contact. We would love to have the opportunity to pray with you and point you to some amazing resources.

MAKING THE EXCHANGE

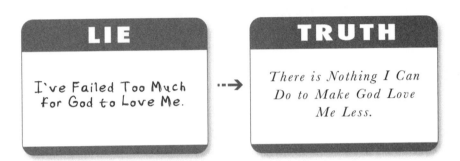

"For as high as the heavens are above the earth, so great is his love for those who fear him; as far as the east is from the west, so far has he removed our transgressions from us." ~ Psalm 103:11-12

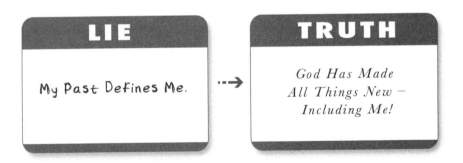

"Therefore, if anyone is in Christ, the new creation has come: The old has gone, the new is here!" ~ 2 Corinthians 5:17

Chapter 6

People-Pleasing

people-pleasing
- [**pee**-*puh* l **plee**-zing]

verb

1. a compulsive behavior that causes one to care too much about what others think of them.
2. a behavior that causes one to strive to make everyone happy, often at the expense of their own-wellbeing.
3. the condition or state of never being able to say "no".
4. see "Ashley Shepherd".

Apparently, "people-pleasing" is not in the dictionary, so my editor wrote the definitions above. Number four is my favorite. Even though this may not be recognized by the dictionary, people-pleasing is a very real struggle that many of us deal with, including myself. Even if you have never dealt with this yourself, it's safe to say you know someone who has.

People-pleasing can appear quite spiritual at first glance. Those who struggles with this may seem like the most giving and spiritual people you know. They are the ones that are at every church event, volunteer for everything, and say "yes" to everyone who asks them for something. Sometimes, this comes from a place of genuine love and care for others, but there are often times when they say "yes," because they are scared to say "no."

For many years, I wore this label like a badge of honor, but the

Lord has taken me on a personal journey of removing it and reclaiming my life, so I can be more effective in the long run and won't burn myself out. My heart in sharing my story in this chapter is for you to not only relate to my story but to my Savior who has and is helping me live free from worry of what others might think.

I truly love people. I enjoy entertaining, hanging out, and spending time with people. I have friends who don't like people half as much as I do, and I just don't understand it. I love hearing people's stories, encouraging women who need hope, and spurring on those who are fighting for their dreams—this is my heart cry. I once took a personality test called StrengthsFinder and discovered I scored high in WOO which stands for "winning others over."

When I meet you or see you for the 679th time, you will get a hug. My husband calls it a "force hug," because I come in, wrap my arms around you, and give you a little squeeze. This can be uncomfortable for some people, but it makes me happy!

I remember how my Papaw Loveday (my dad's father) also loved people and went out of his way to make everyone feel special. There could be 100 other people in the room, but he would make you feel like you were the only one that mattered, and when you left his presence, you would feel valued and loved. Papaw is with Jesus now, but he continues to be someone I model my life after.

My daddy is the same way Papaw was. We were eating out one time recently when our young waitress began calling him "dad" and me "sister." Both my mom and dad have always reminded me that you never know what people go through behind the scenes, and you can sometimes make a dramatic impact in someone's life during what would otherwise be a normal interaction.

For as long as I can remember, I have loved people. In elementary school, I loved making friends, talking to people, and making people laugh. I always got in trouble for talking to other kids during class. (I guess I should lighten up on my son who now gets in trouble for the

People-Pleasing

same thing; it's always hard to punish children for traits you passed down, especially when those traits can be traced back three generations!) I loved playing games outside during recess and desired to be included every time. Looking back, I see that I have always had a desire to gather others and make everyone feel included. I made sure I talked to every single person in my elementary school class! If anyone ever walked by in the hallway, I would wave so they would know I saw them. I was a "noticer" even at a young age. This all seems good, doesn't it?

Don't forget that we have an enemy prowling around, seeking to steal anything he can from our lives (1 Peter 5:8, John 10:10). It wasn't long before the love for people that God had placed in my heart began to get distorted and twisted.

Have you ever noticed that the things God puts inside of us, which shown through when we were children, often get distorted as we enter our teenage and adult years?

....

....

Do you feel like you have ever lost touch with your younger self, as if a part of you got lost along the way? Write down what you feel you have lost. How does this make you feel?

....

....

....

I worked hard to ensure I made the basketball team in middle school. Being a competitive person, I always did my best, but the reality was my primary motivation for joining the team was to socialize and just be a part of the athletic community. I loved the locker room chats, pool parties, and hanging out at practices, and this was all far more important to me than the sport itself, because I felt like I was a part of something.

Have you ever desired to be a part of something bigger than yourself? Why do you think you were drawn to this?

....
....
....

Along the way, I got injured and decided not to pursue basketball as I entered high school. This totally bummed me out! I wanted to feel like I was a part of something, like I had a close group of friends. Since I wasn't on a team, I made sure I was accepted by *everyone*. I thought this was because I loved people—and it was to an extent—but on a much deeper level, I loved being *liked*, and I craved acceptance and affirmation from others in an unhealthy sense.

It wasn't long before I realized that high school was full of cliques. It wasn't like elementary school where you could wave at everyone you passed in the hallway and be friends with the entire school. I didn't particularly like this new environment but continued to be myself in spite of it. Even though I had my tribe, my core friend group who would be with me through anything and still is to this day (you know who you are), my secret mission was to make sure I was loved by *everyone*.

There was, however, one little flaw to my plan. The members of one clique in particular didn't like me, because I was nominated for homecoming queen. When I won, it got worse. This broke my heart and absolutely crushed me. It didn't matter that I had the acceptance of nearly everyone else in the school and wore the crown of homecoming queen, because I felt rejected by one group of girls. I quickly made it my mission to do whatever it took for those girls to like me.

People-Pleasing

Can you relate to the feeling of being rejected by someone? Why do you think you craved the affirmation of those people in the first place?

....
....
....
....

    I tried as hard as I could all through high school, but at the end of the day, I found that I could not make this one group of girls like me no matter how hard I tried. I would overhear things they would say about me, and it would crush my heart into a million pieces. *I don't understand why you don't like me!* I remember thinking. *I am trying so hard; what am I doing wrong?*

    I guess it was my competitive nature that encouraged me to keep trying, facing certain rejection time and time again. It was in those moments that the lies of the enemy began to grow stronger. "You don't belong" and "They don't like you, because you're weird" were thoughts that entered my mind on a regular basis even though I *was* accepted by so many others at my school.

Have you ever felt like you didn't belong? What was your first memory of feeling this way?

....
....
....
....

    Girls can be so cruel. I think almost every woman (and many men) can relate to having similar—or perhaps worse—experiences growing up. I can now see that this experience in high school began a ripple effect that made me even more of a people-pleaser by college. In fact, the main reason why I didn't join a sorority at Middle Tennessee was because I wanted *all* of the sorority girls on campus to like me, and I didn't like the fact that you had to pick one group and stick with them.

It sounds silly as I write this, but as I look back, I can see how the opinions of others dictated my actions. Even though I was popular, I became a people-pleaser who went to great lengths to ensure that I always fit in and was liked.

Perhaps some of you felt like an outcast growing up, and you made people-pleasing your mission, so you would feel included. It's interesting how the same behavior can be caused by different things. We were all wired by God to be loved and to feel like we belong, but there is a tough reality that not everyone will like us. Just because we experience a certain level of rejection doesn't mean we are "rejects." Just because we don't belong everywhere doesn't mean we don't belong anywhere. It simply means there is a space in our hearts that only God can fill.

You may have had different life experiences, and you might care less what others think of you. (If this is you, I'm jealous, because the voices in my head made it seem like the world was coming to an end when I found out someone disliked me.) Regardless of how people-pleasing, the desire to be liked, and the desire to belong has affected your life, I believe that social media has magnified the dysfunction that can arise from these desires if they are not met in healthy ways.

Can we take off our masks for a second and chat about how many things we put on social media, because it makes us look good? How often are we only searching for 'likes' over genuine connection with our friends and family?

Though I actively use social media and enjoy it, I am grateful it didn't exist when I was younger, because I can't imagine how rough high school would've been if I had a social media image to maintain

People-Pleasing

on top of trying to get everyone in the school to like me. The truth is I didn't need social media for the opinions of others to become louder than God's voice, but it has made it worse in my present life.

My sister has four beautiful girls, and I plan to read this chapter to each of them before they enter middle school. I hope that you do the same with the young girls in your life, because in today's world, we need to equip our girls at an early age to fight the battle to not allow the people-pleasing label to stick to their hearts.

Social media can make it easier for me to get caught up in performance and seeking to please others. We all know that everyone uses social media as their highlight reel; I typically won't post videos of my boys fighting over their four-wheeler but will, instead, opt for how handsome they look all dressed up for church on Sunday morning. And I *definitely* don't check back later—certainly not multiple times—to see who 'liked' or commented on my photos so that I can feel valuable.

Come on, be honest, you know you do it, too. In fact, if you think you don't do this, tell me how you feel next time you post something, and hardly anyone 'likes' it. This stuff is addicting, I tell you! It's almost as if social media has put all of us back in high school—the more friends and 'likes' you have the more popular you feel. This is a vicious cycle that requires intentionality to break free.

Even though I know in my heart that other women's social media feeds are their highlight reels, it can be easy for me to fall into the trap of thinking every moment of their lives is as pretty and perfect as it looks on Instagram. I then look at my own life, feel that I don't measure up, and that's where the people-pleasing label can subtly sneak in, as I begin to work and post and tweet and filter until everyone likes me (literally), and I feel like I belong.

When the enemy can get us caring more about what other people think of us than what God thinks of us, he has already begun to steal pieces of our identity. He doesn't have to work too hard to get to this point, because comparison seems to be a trap that most of us easily fall into.

I love the quote, "Comparison is the thief of joy," which was, apparently, originally said by President Teddy Roosevelt. I like to say, "Comparison is an identity thief."

I used to get on social media and see all these women posting photos of gourmet meals they made for their families, and I would think to myself, *Ryan would be better off with one of these women.* I would see couples post about how in love they are and wonder why my marriage didn't look like that. There was even a time when I began to feel like an awful mom, because I didn't do fun stuff with my kids "like all the other moms were doing" on social media. I began to develop a habit of scrolling through my social media feeds just to catch a glimpse of what I thought I could never have which caused me to miss out on what God had put right in front of me. If only I had stopped comparing, so I could see it!

Do you ever compare yourself to others? Why do you think you do this?

....

....

....

I can honestly say this is one of the labels the enemy has used the most to distract me from what God has called me to do. I even held off writing this book for a year after I felt God call me to write it, because I thought no one would want to read it.

People-pleasing has a way of hitting us from both sides. It can cause us to never do things for fear of what people will think (like delaying the writing of this book), but it can also cause us to do things we should *not* be doing, also out of fear of what people will think. People-pleasers can be those who never start things, but they can also be those who take on too much and burn themselves out.

I recently made a list of my priorities in an effort to determine what I should focus on. At the top of the list was my family, followed by the Beautifully Designed ministry and my business. I found that I wasn't really giving these things my all, because I was saying "yes" to everything else around me. From babysitting to volunteering at my kids' school and teaching at church, I didn't know how to say "no" to everyone who asked me to do something, not to mention answering *every* single text and phone call that came through.

The tricky thing was these were all *good* things; they just weren't the things God was calling me to do at this moment in time. But since I didn't know how to say "no," I was engaging in a tug of war with myself, and at the end of the day, I just wanted to hide where no one could find me and add something else to my plate.

When you're driving on a two-lane road, there is a reason why there are two distinct lanes. When two cars meet, they each have a specific lane to stay in, so they don't crash into each other, and they remain focused on their destinations. If you try to drive in the wrong lane—or both lanes—there are going to be problems, and you may not end up getting to where you need to go.

In the same way, God has a specific journey marked out for you, so there's no need to drive all over the road just because the pavement is there. You don't have to pick up the phone every time it rings. You don't have to reply to every text the second it comes in. You don't have to say "yes" to every opportunity even if it seems good and spiritual. This was a very difficult lesson for me to learn, especially with my phone. I ended up having to put it on silent and only check it at designated times, and I eventually got to the point where my phone didn't control my life.

Grab your journal or a piece of paper and make a list of your priorities. What has God called you to do? Who has He called you to take care of? This will help you filter whether or not things are truly a priority, so you can stay in your lane.

On the journey of removing this label, the Lord has allowed me to lose certain friendships, because I valued the opinions of those people more than I did His opinion of me. It hurt me deeply at the moment, but now that I look back, I am grateful that my life is no longer controlled by the opinions of others. Some friendships only last for a season. Your core tribe should be small and consist of people that love you unconditionally and stick with you through thick and thin, despite your imperfections and shortcomings.

I was reading a blog one day when I came across a Scripture that seemed to leap off of my computer screen:

> *Am I now trying to win the approval of human beings, or of God? Or am I trying to please people? If I were still trying to please people, I would not be a servant of Christ* (Galatians 1:10).

Tears began to well up in my eyes, because I knew *my* answer to this question. I realized that this was the reason why my heart was so filled with doubt and insecurity, because I was basing my self-worth on someone else's opinion of what I was doing and how I was doing it.

Why don't you take a moment to answer this question for yourself? Are you living your life to please God or other people in your life?

_____

_____

_____

If this is you, there is hope! You are *not* the only one who has struggled with comparison. In fact, I want to share a story from the Bible that has changed my life forever. In Matthew 14, Jesus was in the midst of His ministry, traveling about with His disciples. He had just finished feeding more than five thousand people with five loaves of bread and two fish (a great story of trusting God to provide when the odds are stacked against us) when it was time to move on to the next thing.

Jesus put the disciples on a boat and sent them to the other side of the lake and went up the mountain to pray. (I love that Jesus took

People-Pleasing

time out to pray and hear from God.) When He was finished, He looked down on the lake and noticed that the boat had drifted far from land, and a storm was brewing. The men were scared, as the boat was tossed back and forth in the wind. (Can you relate to feeling tossed around as though you are alone at sea? It's dark, you can't see Jesus; it's a scary place to be.)

Just before dawn, Jesus came walking on the water. Thinking it was a ghost, the disciples were terrified until the moment they heard Jesus speak, *"Take courage! It is I. Don't be afraid"* (Matthew 14:27).

One of my favorite disciples, Peter, wanted to be sure it was Jesus. He challenged this mysterious stranger who was walking on water: *"Lord, if it's you," Peter replied, "tell me to come to you on the water"* (v. 28). Have you ever had a moment like this where you've asked, "Is this really you, God?"

Jesus responded by telling Peter to come to Him, so Peter got out of the boat and began walking on water. *But when he saw the wind, he was afraid, and beginning to sink, cried out, "Lord, save me!"* (v. 30).

The moment Peter took his eyes off Jesus and began to focus on the wind and the waves crashing around him, he began to sink.

> *Immediately Jesus reached out his hand and caught him. "You of little faith," he said, "why did you doubt?"*
>
> *And when they climbed into the boat, the wind died down. Then those who were in the boat worshiped him, saying, "Truly you are the Son of God"* (v. 31-33).

If you find yourself in the midst of a storm, all you have to do is cry out to Jesus, and He *will* save you! This doesn't always mean that He will take you *out* of the storm; sometimes, it simply means He will take your hand and walk with you *through* it. No matter what you are going through, you can rest assured that Jesus is with you, and He is for you; you are never alone. If you're feeling tossed around in the wind, be still and allow Him to quiet your heart (Zephaniah 3:17).

I lived with the "disease to please" for years, and it left me exhausted and feeling like I wasn't enough. There were so many voices in my head, drowning out the voice of God. I got on my knees one night (there is something about this posture that helps me in surrendering my worries and fears) and cried out to God. I told Him I was tired of worrying about what people thought of me and tired of saying "yes" to everything.

I've put so many things before you, God, I said to myself as I got off my knees and stretched out on my stomach across an ottoman. Tears began to pound the floor as I reached out for God's hand. In that moment, I stopped trying to please myself, and I cried out to God for help, knowing I couldn't keep up the act much longer. As I cried out for God to save me, I felt the wind cease and the noise stop as I grabbed hold of Jesus' hand.

I eventually crawled into bed, my heart quieted and still. I felt hope rising up within me, confident that God would help me. Two weeks later, I went to a conference in Cleveland, Tennessee, that my friends had organized and asked me to help host. To be honest, I almost backed out at the last minute, because my travel schedule was hectic, and I knew I had to finish writing this book and get it sent off to the publisher. (Just the fact that I even *considered* backing out was a miracle; a few years ago, I would have followed through no matter what the cost to emotional health, not to mention my family.) As I pondered what to do, I felt a voice inside of me say, "GO—even if it's hard."

When I arrived at the conference, the first thing they had us do was grab our Bibles and put our phones away. (There was no using that "But I use my phone for the Bible app" excuse.) We began to worship together, raising our voices and our hands to God. We spent some time writing in our journals and some time just sitting in the presence of God. To be honest, I struggled to shut my brain off for the first few hours as thoughts began to bounce around my mind of everything I needed to do the moment I left. I got on my knees and asked God to quiet the voices in my head, so I could hear *His* voice clearly.

People-Pleasing

It wasn't long before I heard God whisper, "You are mine. Will you allow the Holy Spirit to be the only opinion that matters in your life?"

I began to cry so hard that my eyes were nearly swollen shut. I had accepted Jesus as my "personal Savior" years before and knew when I did this that the Holy Spirit came to live inside of me to serve as my "Helper." It even says in John 14:26 that God sent the Holy Spirit to teach us all things and help us to remember everything that Jesus has spoken to us. However, when I felt God whisper that to my heart at the conference in Cleveland, everything I had learned as a little girl suddenly became even more real to me.

I sat on the floor as the worship music and chatter from other women in the room began to fade into the background. It was just me and Jesus, and I was surrendering everything I had been holding onto so tightly. I gave up my "right" to control every aspect of my life and chose to eliminate the noise of the opinions of others. This freed me to focus on what God thought of me and His direction for my life; no longer would I be tossed around by what other people wanted and expected of me.

It was as if Jesus had come to me in the midst of the storm and said, "Take courage! It is I. Don't be afraid." My heart felt so free, and I was able to worship God without being distracted by thoughts of everything I needed to do back at home. I felt a lot like the disciples in the boat, overwhelmed with awe and gratitude for the One who calmed the storm.

I then realized God had answered my prayer from that night on the ottoman. I had been so desperate to hear His voice amidst the noise, and He had responded. It was one thing to read in the Bible that God had given me the Holy Spirit to help me and another thing to actually have the pages of the Bible come alive in *my* life, as God came near and reminded me that His voice was the only voice that truly mattered.

Have you ever struggled to hear God's voice? There have been times when I have wondered if it's really His voice I'm hearing or just my own voice. To be clear, I mostly hear God speak to me through His Word. There are times when I read something in the Bible and just *know* it's for me, because it speaks to my situation. However, I believe that God speaks to us in other ways as well, and my prayer is that I will someday be a Holy Spirit super-agent who often hears whispers from God as I go about my day.

Sometimes, I hear God speak directly to my heart. Jesus said, *"My sheep hear my voice, and I know them, and they follow me"* (John 10:27, ESV). Jesus wasn't referring just to the Bible (which had not even been compiled yet!). Rather, He was referring to having an intimate, personal relationship with Him. This can happen through reading Scripture as the words come alive, and we find God meeting us in the middle of our stories as they become intertwined with His. It's so much more than just reading words in the book, it's having an encounter with the living and active God of the universe.

All throughout the Bible, we hear stories of God interacting with people directly. This was sometimes in the form of a voice, an angel appearing, or even a finger writing on a wall. My point is there are many ways that God speaks, and we shouldn't limit which forms of His communication we desire to hear.

This doesn't mean that every thought that enters into our minds is from God. Not even every word in the Bible is from God (it often records conversations people had amongst themselves and even the words of the enemy!). However, the words we hear God speak directly to us will *always* fall in alignment with the nature and heart of God that we see revealed in Scripture.

One of the ways I know it was God speaking to me and not myself or the enemy were the words themselves. I would not tell myself that God's voice was the only one that mattered with that level of authority, as I was struggling to believe it myself. I also know that the enemy would not tell me that God's voice was the only one that mattered, because he was the one planting lies in my mind in an attempt to get me to believe the opposite!

Another way I know when God is speaking to me is when I receive confirmation of what I feel I heard God say from people I trust. For example, when I felt that God was telling me I needed to write a book, I almost acted as if I didn't hear Him, because it seemed like a daunting task. Within an hour, my mother's mentor of thirty years messaged me and told me I should write a book. She had *no* knowledge of what I had just felt God speak to me an hour before, and I had never mentioned writing a book to her! After that, several other people told me, via text or in person, that I should write a book. It was as if God was leaving a "trail" of evidence of what He was calling me to do.

God did not create you to leave you on your own. He desires to have a relationship with you and communicate with you. What relationship could survive without communication? For those of you who are married, could you imagine living under the same roof as your spouse and never talking to them? What kind of relationship is that?

I have found that God is always speaking. The question is are we listening?

> The topic of learning to hear God's voice is beyond the scope of this book. For further reading, I recommend *Discerning the Voice of God* by Priscilla Shirer. This book changed my life, and I regularly purchase copies to give away to others.

I hope you see how loving and intimate our Heavenly Father is and how much He desires a relationship with you. Having a "relationship" implies that there is interaction, and you communicate with Him, so I pray that you are able to hear His voice above all the noise that has filled your life. When this happens, you'll be able to see what truly matters in life and be able to remove any people-pleasing labels that have stuck to your heart.

Whether you have attended church your whole life, or never stepped foot through the doors, if you have never surrendered your life to Jesus and accepted Him as your Lord and Savior, or if you have accepted Jesus but drifted over time, I invite you to do this today. There is no magic prayer to pray and you don't need to have a pastor present to do this. It can happen right now, no matter where you are or who is around you. It's okay if this is the first time, or if you're simply ready to surrender and grow closer to Jesus than ever before. Regardless of where you've been or what you've done, if you feel Jesus tugging on your heart, get out your laptop or smartphone and go to www.beautifullydesigned.com/MeetJesus.

TAKE A DEEP BREATH

I hope you are beginning to feel the weight of the world falling off of your shoulders. It is time to replace the lies that have held us back with God's truth, so we can fully embrace the freedom that is found only in Jesus Christ.

One thing that is important for you to understand is that you may struggle even after God speaks to you. I had a powerful encounter with God at the conference in Cleveland that did a lot to silence the voice of the enemy and set me free from my people-pleasing ways, but this was only the catalyst in a day-by-day process of removing this label and walking in my true identity. I don't want you to think this was a "one-and-done" event, and I never struggled again, but it was certainly a "defining moment" on my journey, and I'm sure there will be more to follow.

Part of the day-by-day process involves creating new habits. For example, if you've been in the habit of saying "yes" to everything for ten years, it may take you some time to learn to say "no," and you may have to force it the first few times. If you've allowed social media to become a source of comparison that steals your joy, you may need to take a break from social media and use that time to read Scripture instead, or, perhaps, limit the time that you spend on it to once in the morning and once in the evening rather than dozens of times throughout the day. (These are just suggestions; I encourage you to seek the Lord and find what He has for *you* to do to break free from this label and embrace His work in your life.)

The hard truth is that not everyone in this life will like you, and that's okay! We cannot afford to waste time trying to please people who don't genuinely care for us and accept us with all of our flaws and imperfections. Trust me, those are *not* your true friends!

I have also found that the moment we stop trying so hard to fit in and make people like us is the moment we find our place in this world. When we decide to be ourselves and stop trying to be someone else, that is often when we find that there are many people who love us for who we truly are.

MAKING THE EXCHANGE

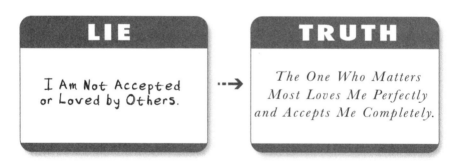

"So that Christ may dwell in your hearts through faith—that you, being rooted and grounded in love, may have strength to comprehend with all the saints what is the breadth and length and height and depth, and to know the love of Christ that surpasses knowledge, that you may be filled with all the fullness of God." ~ Ephesians 3:17-19, ESV

"Accept one another, then, just as Christ accepted you, in order to bring praise to God." ~ Romans 15:7

LIE	TRUTH
I Have to Work Hard to Make People Like Me.	*Pleasing God is More Important than Being "Liked."*

"Am I now trying to win the approval of human beings, or of God? Or am I trying to please people? If I were still trying to please people, I would not be a servant of Christ." ~ Galatians 1:10

Download these Scriptures at www.beautifullydesigned.com/PrintScriptures.

Chapter 7

Self-Worth

self-worth
- [self-wurth]

noun
1. The sense of one's own value or worth as a person; self-esteem; self-respect.

As you can tell, many of the chapters in this book have built on one another and overlapped at points. In this chapter, we will ask the question, "Where do you find your value?" This is a question that has come up in previous chapters, as self-image and self-worth are closely connected, and both of these can come under attack by the shame our failures bring if we don't allow God to tell us how He sees us.

When I was very young, my dad worked as a youth pastor, but that changed one day in 1990 when Papaw bought a campground and asked him to manage it. Dad shifted to doing adult services on Sunday mornings and told Papaw he could manage the campground but only for a short time. I guess God had other plans, because, ultimately, my parents ended up owning that campground and still do to this day!

> If you're ever in Eastern Tennessee,
> the Riverside RV Park and Resort in Sevierville would
> love to have you! (Yes, that is a shameless plug.)
> Find out more at www.riversidecamp.com

The Lord has used this business as a mission field for my parents—instead of them going to people, people come to them! My dad preaches the Gospel in an open-air pavilion each Sunday, and they serve many people throughout the week; it is truly a church without walls.

Mom and Dad also lead a non-profit organization that serves Sevier County Food Ministries (feeding 1,000 families each week) and take ministry trips to an orphanage in San Pedro Sula, Honduras, twice a year. My parents have lived out a life of obedience to God, and I can see the ripple effect in my life and even the lives of my own children.

I loved growing up at the Riverside RV Park, a peaceful oasis at the confluence of the Little Pigeon and French Broad rivers. It was where I learned to ride a bike and worked my first job. It was so much fun to be a part of the family business, especially since I loved people, and we hosted thousands of people each year, with new folks arriving almost daily during the summer. I guess that's where my entrepreneurial spirit was born!

I worked at the park off and on through high school, and Ryan and I decided to move home and help run it after we graduated from MTSU and got married. Our ultimate goal was to travel the world and tell people about Jesus, so it made sense for us to work in the family business even though my degree was in journalism. I worked in the office, Ryan worked outside, and we lived in the mobile home park rent-free. This enabled us to serve on overseas ministry trips and save money for our future.

I took pride in being the owner's daughter and loved greeting everyone and helping them. (Can you see my people-pleasing at work here?) The office workers used to have a friendly competition to see who was better at customer service, which I loved. At the same time, I sometimes wondered if I had settled in my career, because working in the family business was pretty much the easiest job for me to get. I watched as my friends landed their dream jobs—or at least jobs where

Self-Worth

they were using their degrees—and I grew discouraged. I questioned if we had made the right choice in moving home, even if it did enable us to move toward our dream of having the freedom to travel.

Wondering if I was in the right career, I quickly became a "serial applicant." Seriously, I applied for more than 75 jobs and was rejected by every single one, because I didn't have enough "experience," which I didn't understand, because I was a new graduate—how are we supposed to get experience if no one will hire us?! I even applied to HGTV corporate in Knoxville, and they turned me down! Come on y'all, if there's one thing I'm good at, it's decorating!

Here I was, in my early 20s just graduated from college, newly married—you would think I had everything going for me, but I felt hopelessly stuck in the in-between. I was no longer a college girl, but I didn't feel like an adult, because it felt like I didn't have a "real job." This led to many nights where I felt unsettled. I didn't understand why I felt this way at the time, but when I look back, I know exactly why I felt this way; I was finding my self-worth in my job. Since I didn't yet have a "career job," I felt as though I wasn't valuable which began to undermine my identity.

Have you ever struggled with allowing your job or career to define you?

....
....
....
....

If I could go back in time, I would tell the younger Ashley Shepherd to find her value in who she *is* not in what she *does*. This is so tricky, especially in a society that places such a strong emphasis on what we "do." Think about it; what is one of the first questions we typically ask when meeting someone? So, *what do you do?*

It's important to work to provide for your family, and most families aren't lucky enough to be able to live on one income. However, we can't allow our jobs to become *the* thing that defines us; we must find our sense of value, security, and identity in Christ. When our identity is rooted in Christ, and we allow Him to be the one to define us, what we "do" becomes secondary.

When we become defined by our jobs, we can become prideful when we are successful at work and be driven to despair when things aren't going so well or when we lose our jobs altogether. I don't know about you, but I don't want to find my ultimate purpose and value in something that can change or be taken from me so easily.

I think of my sister, Keeli, who has worked in human resources for her entire career. She perfected her skills over the past fifteen years and successfully climbed the corporate ladder in a male-dominated workforce. (She is the smart one in our family!) She recently received the coveted title of HR vice president, only to learn shortly thereafter, that the company where she had worked for twelve years was bought out. In a moment, her identity was stripped away. She went from being the glue that held the place together to the one that would have to let every employee go, with herself being the last to be shown the door.

I remember seeing her one morning, her eyes still puffy from crying herself to sleep the night before. I saw the hurt in her eyes and even in the way she walked, no longer confident and full of life. She felt lost, unsure of who she was. She had felt valued in her career, because she was good at what she did, she was the one that everyone came to when they had a problem, the one who could solve everyone's problems, but all of that was gone. She was no longer Keeli Boyce, HR Vice President, so what was her purpose in life? What was she supposed to do after spending two decades building something that was gone in a moment? I wanted desperately to take her pain away, but I knew there was nothing I could do in the short term to restore her sense of self-worth that had been lost.

Perhaps you have experienced the same thing and can feel her pain, or maybe you are like me and just didn't feel like you knew where you belonged, as though you hadn't quite found your place in the world. Regardless of your experience, it's important that you ask yourself where you are getting your sense of value. Your job isn't what makes you you. It may teach you valuable lessons and introduce you to some amazing people, but it's not the totality of who you are, and it was never supposed to be. So many of us give everything we have to our jobs, only to end up lost and confused when they don't provide us with the sense of fulfillment we crave. I have found that even when I am successful at something, I always want *more* until I rest my identity in Christ and allow my relationship with Him to fulfill me and provide my sense of value and self-worth.

It took Keeli a year to rise up above the fog, but she is a fighter, and she pulled through. She joined a great company and built a new team from the ground up, Express Strategic Services. In her words, "We partner with clients to enhance human resource management and digital marketing concepts that align with the strategic and long-term goals of their organization."

Some of you may not be able to relate to Keeli's story at all, because raising kids is your "full-time job." But even this is a place where we can misplace our value. Placing our value in our degrees, careers, marriages, or kids is easy to do. If you get your sense of self-worth from your kids, what happens when your kids, inevitably, leave to begin their own lives? I have known many women who have felt like they have no purpose in life when their kids leave home. And what happens if, God forbid, your kids don't make the best choices as adults? While you can certainly point them in the right direction, you can't run their lives for them, and if your identity is wrapped up in your kids, you will blame yourself if their lives don't turn out the way you thought they would.

In addition to defining ourselves by these labels, we are quick to place labels on each other. *She's a stay-at-home mom, working mom, work-from-home mom, breastfeeding mom, bottle-feeding mom, cloth-diaper mom, homeschool mom.* The list goes on and on. We put each other in little boxes and assign value accordingly. To some, a mom who stays at home with her kids is inherently better than a working mom, and to others, the opposite is true.

I'll never forget the time I told a friend I had stopped breastfeeding my son, and she looked at me as if I had told her I had stopped feeding him entirely! I did not understand this, as I felt I had made the best choice for both my son and my sanity. In disgust, she stuck the label "bottle-feeding mom" on me for everyone to see.

I have news for you; a woman's value is *not* found in what she decides to do with her life! We need to stop categorizing one another and, instead, help each other rip off the labels that have defined us and find our true value in Christ. I don't write this to make anyone feel ashamed or guilty.

If we're honest, we've *all* done this to one another—sometimes without realizing it. (I think this is because we have all had our own experiences, and we subconsciously assume that everyone else has had the same experiences that we have and, therefore, share our opinions.) Most of us have labeled one another unintentionally, but we can counteract this by being intentional to help others remove the labels that have been placed on them. This begins once we have removed the labels from our own hearts, so we can take others by the hand and show them how to remove the labels from theirs. The only way to accomplish this is to point them to Christ and live out the example in front of them.

God did not create us for uniformity but to embrace the uniqueness of how He designed us.

Have you ever felt like you didn't measure up to someone else, because you made different decisions for yourself or your family? If you have, how did that make you feel?

....

....

....

....

Self-Worth

What do you think God wants to say to you about this?

_____
_____
_____
_____

In our culture, we measure a person's value in all sorts of ways: their careers, where they live, how much money they make, where their kids go to school, etc. Many of us are exhausted from repeated attempts at "keeping up with the Jones'." Social media makes this even worse, because it's so easy to look at someone else's "success" and compare our lives to them. We look at their highlight reels and begin to question what we have done wrong and why we aren't as far along in life as they are. In this process, we label both ourselves and them, and this often isn't even grounded in reality—it's just from the "outside image" we see on the Internet.

This is also what causes us to drive by houses and ask ourselves, "What do these people do for a living?" which is often followed with, "Why didn't I do that?" We see their beautiful homes, cars, kids, and vacations, and jealousy begins to pierce our hearts. Placing our self-worth in these things causes us to become unsettled and discontent with what God has already given us.

One of my favorite Bible verses is *I can do all this through him who gives me strength* (Philippians 4:13). This verse fills my heart with hope, and I pray it does yours as well!

If you look back at the verses immediately before it, you'll see there is a deeper meaning here: *...for I have learned to be content whatever the circumstances. I know what it is to be in need, and I know what it is to have plenty. I have learned the secret of being content in any and every situation, whether well fed or hungry, whether living in plenty or in want. I can do all this through him who gives me strength* (Philippians 4:11b-13).

Other translations of this verse say, "I can do *all things* through him who strengthens me" (ESV). But when we see the context, we see that the Apostle Paul isn't saying God will give us some sort of superhuman strength, so we can, literally, do *anything*, but that God will give us the strength to be content no matter what situation we find ourselves in: whether we have more than enough or are barely getting by, whether we live in our dream house or the poor house, whether we have a refrigerator full of food or need help buying groceries. In every situation, God will take care of us and give us the strength we need to be content and not compare ourselves to anyone else.

Ouch, that hurts a bit, especially when we live in a culture that has spiritualized the American Dream. The truth is God doesn't automatically "bless" us with a big house and high-paying jobs when we give our lives to Him. This stuff is nice, but God's greatest blessings are things that money cannot buy, so we can't compare ourselves to someone else and ask, "God, why haven't you blessed *me* like you have *them?*"

There have been seasons in my life when I had to call Ryan while shopping to make sure we had enough money in our checking account if I added an extra item to my cart. When I would see others that didn't have a financial worry in the world, I would grow frustrated. This is because I was placing my self-worth in our finances. When our bank balance was down, I was down. Let's be real, we all want to be successful financially, but chasing the American Dream should not take hold of our lives to the point where we value it over the One who created and owns everything.

My family recently took a vacation to Punta Mita, Mexico. I was working on this book outside one night, the gentle breeze of the ocean blowing across my face as the waves crashed in the background. I remember praying and asking God what He wanted me to write, but not long after, I began to feel insecure as I wondered what those who read it would think of my writing.

My heart through this whole process has been to write what I felt God was putting on my heart, so it's interesting that as I was writing about finding our self-worth in Jesus, I began to feel that mine was tied to whether or not people like what I write. Isn't it funny how God teaches us these lessons in the process of ministering to others?

One definition of "value" is "the importance, worth, or usefulness of something." I want you to make a list of the things you value most in life. This will help you determine if there is anything you hold in higher value than God. Don't worry; I am doing this with you, and I already wrote down "the opinions of others about my book" on my list.

What is most important in your life? Is it your job, spouse, kids, sports, or your hobbies?

In order to help you discover what is truly most important to you, write down the five things that took up the bulk of your time in the last week:

Now, I understand most of us have to work twenty-five to forty hours a week or raise a family, and we likely aren't going to spend forty hours a week reading the Bible. This doesn't necessarily mean you value your job or family over God, so let's dig a little deeper.

What consumed your thoughts last week? To what did you give the bulk of your physical, mental, and emotional energy?

The Bible says,

Whatever you do, work at it with all your heart, as working for the Lord, not for human masters, since you know that you will receive an inheritance from the Lord as a reward. It is the Lord Christ you are serving (Colossians 3:23-24).

Work is a gift from God (including the "work" of raising a family which is often much more than 40 hours a week!). In this Scripture, we see what our attitude should be toward work. We should give it our all, even if it feels like what we're doing isn't very spiritual, because it is actually the Lord we are serving. (So, if you don't like your boss, just pretend they are Jesus, and do just as good of a job for them as you would for Him!)

I also like how it says "as working for the Lord, not for human masters." In other words, our highest aim should be to please God not people. We should work to bring God glory and get our value from our relationship with Him, rather than striving to please people and get our sense of value from how well we perform in our jobs.

This is what this whole chapter is about, and it brings us such freedom. If your job feels boring or unspiritual, remember that it is God who you are working for! And if you ever fail, it doesn't mean you *are* a failure, because it is not your work that gives you your sense of self-worth or what defines you. God is the One who defines you; He is the One you are working to please. All He asks is that you put your heart into what you're doing (this means that you also have a positive attitude while you're doing it!), and in that you will bring Him glory.

Now that we've addressed work, let's talk about what we do with the rest of our time. We all have 168 hours each week, and we've only addressed 40 hours. Now, I'm sure you also sleep. (Who doesn't love sleep?!) Let's be super idealistic and say you sleep 8 hours each night. That's 56 hours a week that you're asleep for a total of 96 hours. Now, here's the thing: You still have a whopping 72 hours left in your week. So, don't try to make excuses that you're "too busy at work" to carve out time for the Lord. Even if you spend an extra 28 hours a week (4 hours a day) taking care of your home or family, you've still got 44 hours left—the equivalent of another full-time job! What are you giving that time to?

I'm not asking you to give the "right," churchy answer. Don't write down that you pray for 6 hours a day if you don't. God isn't interested in you putting on a show; He just wants your heart. Let's take work, sleep, raising kids, and all of those other things you "have"

Self-Worth

to do out of the picture and evaluate what you do with the rest of your time:

_____
_____
_____
_____

You will make time for what you value. Period. No if's, and's, or but's! If it is important to you, you will make it a priority.

Was gathering with other believers, reading your Bible, serving your community, or spending time with God in prayer and worship on your list?

_____
_____

I'm not trying to put any shame labels on you if these things haven't been priorities in your life. I simply desire to help you prioritize what *truly* matters, so you can live an abundant life with no regrets. When you grab hold of what truly matters most in life, you can let go of the things you have been prioritizing to please others and the things you have been giving yourself to in order to fill the emptiness you felt in your soul (such as excessive amounts of Netflix and Oreos).

There was a time in my life when I valued TV shows a *lot*. I would DVR the fire out of *Amazing Race* and *The Voice* but make little time to hear God's voice and experience His amazing grace. I remember putting the boys to bed and plopping down on the couch, excited to spend *hours* watching my shows. This took my mind off my own insecurities and depression, as I lived vicariously through watching other people chase *their* dreams.

One of my mentors challenged me to turn the TV off and find something else to do with my evenings, something more "productive." I thought she was nuts. *Doesn't she understand that these shows are my way of escaping reality?!* Looking back, I think she understood that perfectly. She knew that I was finding my sense of self-worth in watching the lives of others, though I was drowning in doubts and insecurities on the other side of the screen. I craved excitement and connection, and I got that from watching people race around the world—but at the end of each episode, I had to press "play" on another to keep those feelings alive. At the end of the night, I would crawl into bed alone (because Ryan was traveling for work) and feel completely empty. I would even ask God if He was ever going to use me to do anything great for His Kingdom. How in the world could God even get my attention when I valued *The Voice* over being still and listening for His voice!

Another area where I have felt the Lord convict me recently is how much time I spend on social media. I don't like this. I've made excuses and reminded God that I "need" to be on Facebook as much as I am, because "my ministry is on there." In reality, I was more obsessed with Facebook than God's word or my own kids, and I was missing out on all of the ways God was speaking to me in my actual life. You never know when the Holy Spirit is going to lead you to pay for a stranger's meal or pick up the phone and call a friend. By allowing margin in our schedules, we make space for what God might want to do in us and through us.

TAKE A DEEP BREATH

Over the course of the next week, I want you to take a time audit. I'll be honest and tell you up front that I do not like doing these, because I realize how much time I spend on things that aren't helping me reach my goals in life.

You often hear people say, "I don't have enough time," when a look at their social media feed shows they spent two days sitting around the house. This is the excuse we use when we have invested the bulk of our time in things that aren't moving us forward. There is a time and a place for everything, and downtime should be a part of our routines, but we tend to cram our schedules so full of stuff at the front end of the week that we are lethargic and in a mental fog by the end of the week.

To complete your time audit, grab a blank piece of paper (the kind with lines works best). Each day, write down everything you do and the time frame in which you do it. For example:

9:00-11:00am — Cleaned the house
11:00-11:30am — Scrolled through Facebook
11:30-Noon — Lunch

I believe the Lord is always at work among us, but we often miss what He is doing, because we don't value our time enough to be good stewards of it. It may be a bit tedious to track everything you do for a week, but it is very important. You can't fix something if you don't know what is wrong with it. This exercise will help you take control of your schedule and redeem your time, so it is not consumed by things that, ultimately, leave you feeling empty. At the end of the day, you'll find that you actually have *more* time for the things you hold the closest to your heart.

"Wake up, sleeper, rise from the dead, and Christ will shine on you." Be very careful, then, how you live—not as unwise but as wise, making the most of every opportunity, because the days are evil (Ephesians 5:14-16).

What is your life? You are a mist that appears for a little while and then vanishes (James 4:14b).

I don't know about you, but I don't want to waste my life watching other people live their dreams and never live my own. I want to be in the fight, be entirely engaged in life. I want to make a positive impact on every person I come into contact with each and every day; I want to make a difference in the lives of others. I want to make memories with Wilson and Levi, wear the bathing suit, and go on hikes. I want to sit back and watch my boys play with their daddy in the backyard. I love to hear their laughs as they wrestle, see their smiles as they pin him to the ground. I believe these are moments when God gives us little glimpses of Heaven.

The sight of a newborn baby, the smile of a child who just lost their first tooth, the graduations that come and go so quickly as this great big world keeps spinning faster and faster. At the end of the day, what remains? Is it your job, your career, your houses, your cars? Or is it your relationship with God, your family, your close friends, all those you love?

Life can be here one day and gone the next. It's just a vapor, a fleeting breath—so we might as well breathe in deeply and fully embrace it. Every moment is precious; make yours count.

MAKING THE EXCHANGE

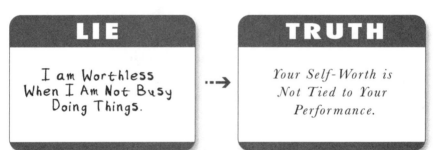

"Whatever you do, work at it with all your heart, as working for the Lord, not for human masters, since you know that you will receive an inheritance from the Lord as a reward. It is the Lord Christ you are serving." ~ Colossians 3:23-24

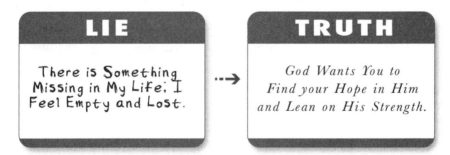

For God alone, O my soul, wait in silence, for my hope is from him. He only is my rock and my salvation, my fortress; I shall not be shaken. ~ Psalm 62:5-6

Chapter 8

Daughter

daughter
- [daw-ter]

noun
1. A girl or woman in relation to either or both of her parents.
2. A female descendant.
3. A woman considered as the product of a particular person, influence, or environment.
4. Something far, far deeper.

Over the last seven chapters, we have been on a journey of discovering our true identity in Christ. The heart behind this book is to gently remind you who you are—God's daughter.

When most people hear the word "daughter," they immediately think of that girl's parents. She is the product of them, of their influence and their environment. Most daughters end up resembling their parents in many ways, even those that try to be nothing like their parents.

I'm proud to be the daughter of Kent and Teresa Loveday. They were a positive influence and excellent role models; I wouldn't trade them for anyone else. Parents play many roles, but I think the one that meant the most to me was my parents providing a sense of security. You know, the security you feel when you get hurt on the playground, and your mom fixes you up and gives you a big hug or when your boyfriend breaks up with you, but your dad comforts you and reminds you just how beautiful you are. The security you feel when you just lost your job but can pick up the phone and, in a moment, feel like everything is going to be alright.

As amazing as my parents are, I have learned over the years that I am even more proud of being a daughter of the King of Kings, Jesus Christ. And I truly desire to be a product of His influence in my life.

Now, I understand not all of you had wonderful parents. As you read the last few paragraphs, you may have found yourself thinking, *Good for you, Ashley, but I have never experienced that.*

If you find yourself feeling this way, the good news is you *do* have a Father in Heaven who loves you perfectly and completely. We were all born with a desire to feel safe. Our Heavenly Father, the King of Kings, is the only one who can truly satisfy this desire.

No matter what you may have gone through growing up, you do not have to be a product of your environment; you can be a product of *His* environment which is full of love, joy, peace, patience, kindness, goodness, faithfulness, gentleness, and self-control (Galatians 5:22-23).

Being a daughter of the King means *you* are royalty! You are deeply loved, adored, valued, and safe in God's arms. He is your advocate and defender. He also gives you power through the Holy Spirit (Acts 1:8) to live victoriously and overcome every scheme of the enemy. You were born for greatness.

How do you feel about the idea that you are royalty? Does it feel like it's true? Why or why not?

....

....

....

....

A tangible example of this is superhero movies. There's something exhilarating about watching the heroes—who often start out

Daughter

as somewhat ordinary—recognize that they were born for greatness. I love watching them rise up and become who they were destined to be. I love how they get a cool outfit, awesome weapons, and a fun sidekick to help them save the day. What makes this even better is that these heroes are usually the underdogs that have to beat the odds to defeat the enemy. In the process, they realize their true identity as mighty warriors.

These are fun movies to watch, especially with my boys. In fact, this is one of the reasons why I am grateful that God gave me two boys! It just makes it easier to walk into a theater to watch a movie meant for kids if I've got one on each arm, rather than being by myself. Wilson and Levi will yell with excitement at the high points of the movie, because they want the hero to win. Part of me wants to yell with them, but I know I have to be the responsible one and tell them to hush so that everyone else can enjoy the movie. (Sometimes, I pretend I wasn't screaming with them!)

Do you like movies or TV shows where someone rises up and does something they were born to do? There is a reason for this. It is because of how God designed you! In this life, there are things that God has given you to do that will require you to rise up, beat the odds, and overcome adversity. In doing this, you will bring freedom and hope to others and realize your true identity. Sounds exciting, doesn't it?!

In real life, you won't always save the day like the heroes in the movies do 99.9 percent of the time. There will be times when your giant defeats you, and you can't go on, but part of life is learning from your failures, refusing to allow them to define you, and rising up to take on the next challenge in spite of your past.

This is the very reason why I have written this book. The enemy is a huge giant, and his goal is to make us feel so defeated that we shrink back and never try again. He seeks to attach so many labels to us that we don't recognize who God created us to be and live inferior and unfulfilling lives rather than stepping into what God has for us.

I'm working on this final chapter late at night while the rest of my family sleeps. I can picture countless women across the world right now, asleep in their beds, completely unaware that there are giants lurking in their thoughts. Hundreds of thousands of women defeated by the storms of life, past hurts, and present insecurities. I see these giants slipping into the cracks of every marriage, friendship, and family, slithering their way into the hearts of every woman, so they feel isolated and confused as to why they have to suffer alone.

Are you one of these women, unsure of how to fight the battle that rages around you? Why do you think this is the case?

_____
_____
_____

We all look for a superhero to face and defeat our giants. We need someone who is fierce, someone who is not afraid. Have you ever thought that this "someone" just might be you?

You may currently be wearing labels that call you a failure, a people-pleaser, or one with low self-esteem. You may be drowning in shame that causes you to think God couldn't possibly work through you. No matter what your circumstances, you need to know that you have everything you need to face this giant. You have been given a courageous heart. You may not *feel* like this is the case, but it is time to awaken your inner warrior and take a stand against the schemes of the enemy.

What does a warrior look like? A warrior is someone who fights in battles and is known for her skills and courage. She is able to silence the voices in her head that tell her she "can't" to try to keep her down. Her words and actions match up; she is a woman of her word. She is a servant who puts others before herself. She doesn't wear a mask but is authentic and transparent, though she is imperfect.

This is *you*. It's always been you. You were born for greatness, you have been given a courageous heart, and you are never alone in any battle or storm. We can often lose sight of these realities due to our circumstances, so it is important that we remind ourselves and each other of our true identity as daughters of the King. You can probably think back to when you were a fierce young girl with the world at your fingertips. You weren't scared of challenges or the opinions of others; you overcame them with great bravery. Imagine you are that girl right now—your arms stretched wide, ready to tackle what God has for you, knowing you have what it takes inside of you. You are still that girl; if only you can see it.

Along the way, many of us have forgotten how to fight or, perhaps, become too weary from the battle and given up. There is a warrior in the Bible who I believe we can learn from. His name is King David. (Perhaps you have heard of him...?) Like many of us, David was an ordinary person who God chose to do extraordinary things. Let's pick up the story in 1 Samuel, before he became king:

> *The Lord said to Samuel, "How long will you mourn for Saul, since I have rejected him as king over Israel? Fill your horn with oil and be on your way; I am sending you to Jesse of Bethlehem. I have chosen one of his sons to be king"* (1 Samuel 16:1).

You see, Saul was the current king over Israel, but things weren't going so well. In fact, the verse immediately before the one above tells us that God regretted that He had made Saul king (1 Samuel 15:35). So, he spoke to his prophet, Samuel, and gave him pointed, yet counterintuitive, instructions. God told Samuel to go to a specific person in a specific place and to take his horn of oil with him, because he was going to anoint a new king to lead Israel.

Samuel balked at first. "I can't do that!" he said. "Saul is still king. If he finds out I'm trying to undermine his authority, he'll have me killed" (16:2).

The Lord quickly reassured Samuel, giving him further instructions but stopping short of the full picture. *I will show you what to do, Samuel.* (16:3)

Has this ever happened to you? Have you ever felt God leading you to do something, only to immediately think, *I can't possibly do that?* If so, you're in good company!

The next verse simply tells us, *Samuel did what the Lord said* (16:4). So simple, yet so profound. Samuel willingly did something that scared him, with only a few instructions from God and a promise that He would show him what else he needed to do when the moment arrived. He got over his fear of what Saul might think of him and decided to obey God.

If we're honest, this wouldn't be most of us. We would want the full picture *and* be able to control the situation. (I have never struggled with this personally, although I'm sure *you* have. Hehe! I think you know me better than that by this point.)

God has a way of only telling us things as we need to know them. I see this in Scripture as well as in my own life. I think it's because if God gave us the full picture all at once, we could take it and do it on our own, leaving Him behind. God wants to not only be on the journey *with* us; He wants to be the one to *guide* us.

When Samuel arrived in Bethlehem, Jesse brought his sons before him. Samuel saw Eliab, who was probably the best and the brightest, and thought to himself, *He must be the one God has in mind* (v. 6).

No sooner had the thought crossed his mind than God spoke to Samuel,

> *"Do not consider his appearance or his height, for I have rejected him. The Lord does not look at the things people look at. People look at the outward appearance, but the Lord looks at the heart"* (v. 7).

First off, I love how God referred to Himself in the third person. He's definitely cool enough to do that. Second, I love the line that says, *The Lord does not look at the things people look at.* That certainly rips a few labels off! Good-bye shame, failure, people-pleasing, and negative self-image. God was not looking for a man who *looked* the most like a warrior but a man who had the *heart* of a warrior.

How often have you thought that you can't do something because of your physical appearance?

Jesse had seven of his sons stand in front of Samuel, and each time God whispered, "This isn't the one."

Samuel said to him, "The Lord has not chosen these. So he asked Jesse, "Are these all the sons you have?" (v. 10b-11a).

"Well," Jesse replied, scratching his head. "There is the youngest, but he is busy taking care of my sheep" (v. 11b).

Can you hear the skepticism in Jesse's reply? He clearly didn't think very highly of his youngest son, because he hadn't even bothered to go out into the field to get him when the prophet arrived, even though this son was the one who was serving the others and protecting the family flock.

Samuel said, "Send for him; we will not sit down until he arrives" (v. 11c).

I can imagine Samuel was frustrated at this point. Perhaps he even questioned if this was really what God had called him to do. Why would God send him all the way to Bethlehem, cycle through all of Jesse's best sons, and none of them be the right fit? Obviously, this shepherd boy wasn't going to be a better option.

Do you ever get impatient with God when you feel like you have heard Him clearly and been obedient, but there are delays in the process? How can you trust God more in the midst of life's delays?

The next part of the story tells us that Jesse sent for his youngest son. When Samuel saw David, the Scripture says, *He was glowing with health and had a fine appearance and handsome features* (v. 12b). So why in the world didn't Jesse bring him along with the rest of his boys in the first place?!

Seconds later, Samuel heard God say, *"Rise and anoint him; this is the one"* (v. 12c).

So Samuel took the horn of oil and anointed him in the presence of his brothers, and from that day on the Spirit of the Lord came powerfully upon David (v. 13).

Think about that for a moment. *From that day on, the Spirit of the Lord came powerfully upon David.* He didn't just have a moment when God's Spirit was on him, it never ended. If we read the rest of David's story, we see that he screwed up epically years down the road, but he had a humble heart, and God's Spirit remained on him.

I hope this brings you as much comfort as it does me! No matter what you may go through, no matter how many times you may get knocked down, the Spirit of the Lord is upon you if you have accepted Jesus as your Savior. When you struggle and fall, you don't have to start the whole process over; you just need to remember your true identity and get back up!

The book of 1 Samuel tells us that David ended up serving Saul even though he was anointed to replace him! That must have required a lot of humility, to serve someone else when you knew in your heart that you belonged in their position. David remained in the shadows for some time, until a literal giant named Goliath began to threaten the people of Israel. Saul and the rest of the army was dismayed and terrified (1 Samuel 17:11). Goliath continued to taunt them for four days, with no one standing up to him.

During this time, David was taking care of his father's sheep while his brothers were on the front lines of Saul's army. (No wonder God didn't choose them as king; they were among the "terrified" ones!) One day, Jesse sent David to take some food to his brothers. When he reached the battlefield and saw the giant that his people were up against, he offered to take him on.

David said to Saul, "Let no one lose heart on account of this Philistine; your servant will go and fight him" (v. 32).

Not only did that take courage, it shows us David's humility once again. Even though he was Saul's *replacement*, he called himself his *servant*. David knew that he was a warrior even though he had not yet had any action on the battlefield.

Saul replied, "You are not able to go out against this Philistine and fight him; you are only a young man, and he has been a warrior from his youth" (v. 33).

Oh please! "You are not able"—are you kidding me?! Saul clearly did not know that God's Spirit was upon David and that God Himself was the source of his strength. In fact, while taking care of his father's sheep, David had faced off against a lion and a bear and defeated both!

But David said to Saul, "Your servant has been keeping his father's sheep. When a lion or a bear came and carried off a sheep from the flock, I went after it, struck it and rescued the sheep from its mouth. When it turned on me, I seized it by its hair, struck it and killed it (v. 34).

Keep in mind that this is the youngest and likely the weakest of Jesse's boys who, from the outside, was the last choice to become king. God clearly had other plans! (We won't fully dive into this story within the pages of this book, but I encourage you to open your Bible to 1 Samuel 16-17 and follow along. The whole story is absolutely incredible!)

I guess David's speech was pretty convincing, because all Saul could muster in response was, *"Go, and the Lord be with you"* (v. 37b). I imagine he said it more like, "Go ahead, David. I hope God is with you, because you're about to face a giant that no one else has the courage to face."

David was the underdog by a longshot, but he had been anointed by God and prepared for this moment. Before he faced his big giant in public, he had faced smaller giants (the lion and the bear) in private. He defeated these animals to save the lives of his sheep, and he defeated Goliath to save an entire nation.

What giants are you facing today?

_____
_____
_____

Do you feel like you are the underdog in this battle? How can you rely on the Lord's strength to face these giants?

_____
_____
_____

Have you ever thought that perhaps the "small" giants you face are simply preparation for larger giants you will face in the future? How does defeating these giants impact your own life and the lives of others?

_____
_____
_____

After Saul caved and allowed David to go up against Goliath, he dressed him in his armor. This was the king's armor, but it was not *the* King's armor. Like a child wearing his older brother's clothes that are too big and baggy, Saul's armor did not fit David (v. 38-39).

David ripped off the uncomfortable armor of the earthly king and decided instead to rely on the King of Kings to protect him. All he had was a staff, slingshot, and a shepherd's bag, which I imagine was somewhat like today's fanny-pack. David went down to a gently-flowing stream and picked up five small stones that were worn smooth by the waters. He put these stones in his fanny-pack and walked out onto the battlefield to face Goliath, without a stitch of armor on (v. 40).

You can pick up the story in 1 Samuel 17:41-51. David stood before Goliath, a giant wearing the finest armor who even had an errand boy to hold his shield for him (v. 41), totally unprepared and unqualified if it were not for the favor of God on his life. Goliath began to mock him while David responded in a calm and collected manner, matter-of-factly telling Goliath that he was going to defeat him and cut off his head and that God was going to help him do it.

I know this sounds totally morbid, and of course, God does not want us to literally do this to our enemies (i.e. the last woman who gave you a nasty look). This story is symbolic of how God will give us the strength to defeat the enemy who is trying to label us and, ultimately, defeat us. You may seem totally unprepared for this battle, but you don't need any type of special training or armor. All you need is confidence in who your God is and who He has created you to be!

Let's dig a little deeper and define your giants. What is the name of the giant you are facing today?

I'm going to do this with you. My giant is called **Insecurity** *. Now, let's dig a little deeper. I can say, "I'm just insecure" and try to muster up my own strength to be confident and overcome these insecurities. Or, I can get to the root of the problem. The truth is the reason why I am insecure is because I know I've gained weight, and I don't want other people to see me. The label I'm wearing is "self-image," but the root cause of my worrying about my self-image is actually people-pleasing. I know I've gained weight, and I'm worried about what other people will think of me.*

In order to have victory over your giants, you have to know where they came from, how they attack you. What labels are you wearing, and what are the root causes that have caused those labels to become giants in your life?

Goliath was covered in armor, but there was one area of his body that had no armor—his forehead. That is where David took aim with his slingshot and struck him with a stone, in the one area where the giant was weak.

Do your giants have any weaknesses?

What strategy is God giving you to attack these giants where they are weak?

This will look different for everyone, but one example may be when your giant begins to lie to you, telling you all of these things that do not line up with who you are. You can respond with the truth of who God says you are. When your giant says, "You are weak and can never defeat me!" you can respond, "I am more than a conqueror through Christ!" (Romans 8:37).

Once you have identified the way the enemy attacks you, the

root cause of your labels, the enemy's weaknesses, and how you can defeat him, you have a decision to make. Will you stand and fight or cower in fear?

When David faced his giant, he boldly told him, "I'm going to defeat you." In the same way, we must face our giants and boldly declare that we are going to defeat them through Christ. It's not our power but the power of Christ in us, so don't worry if you have doubts as to whether or not this is even possible. Make the decision to rise up and trust God to give you the strength you need to overcome your greatest giants.

Once you rise up and face your giants, you will almost certainly be met with opposition. When David first arrived on the battlefield and saw that everyone was terrified of Goliath, he overheard some men talking about a reward that Saul was offering for anyone who could defeat him. When he turned to the men to ask about the reward, his oldest brother, Eliab, overheard him and asked, "What are you doing here? Why aren't you watching the sheep, where you belong? You are so arrogant to think *you* could take on Goliath!" (1 Samuel 17:28).

What a confidence boost! Have you ever had a family member—perhaps an older sibling—tell you that you can't do something? It hurts when those closest to you don't support you. This was reflected in David's response to his brother, *"Now what have I done?" said David. "Can't I even speak?"* (v. 29). Some of you have had this exact experience when it feels like you can't even ask a simple question without someone finding something wrong with it.

I love how David responded after he said this. Instead of getting into an argument with his brother, David turned to another man and repeated his initial question. He totally ignored the negative voices and didn't feel the need to prove who he was. He was already anointed king and knew his true identity, without feeling the need to people-please. His brother was trying to tear him down, but David chose to rise up and take the high road.

Whatever you focus on grows larger. When we're hit with negativity, we cannot give it a voice in our lives or it will grow larger than God's voice. This doesn't just mean we stick our fingers in our ears and pretend we can't hear the negative voices. David heard the voice of his brother and started to respond but stopped short. In the same way, we can physically hear negativity but choose not to give it more air time in our hearts than it deserves.

At the end of the day, the battle belongs to the Lord (v. 47). When people say negative things to you or criticize you behind your back, give it to the Lord and allow Him to be your defense. You don't need to get caught up in proving yourself or pleasing others, because you belong to God and are confident in what He put inside of you, even if other people fail to recognize it.

TAKE A DEEP BREATH

As David faced off against Goliath, the giant began to taunt him.

> *He looked David over and saw that he was little more than a boy, glowing with health and handsome, and he despised him. He said to David, "Am I a dog, that you come at me with sticks?" And the Philistine cursed David by his gods. "Come here," he said, "and I'll give your flesh to the birds and the wild animals!"* (v. 42-44).

Yeah. Just a little intense.

> *David said to the Philistine, "You come against me with sword and spear and javelin, but I come against you in the name of the Lord Almighty, the God of the armies of Israel, whom you have defied. This day the Lord will deliver you into my hands, and I'll strike you down and cut off your head." ... "All those gathered here will know that it is not by sword or spear that the Lord saves; for the battle is the Lord's, and he will give all of you into our hands"* (v.45-47).

Do you see how confident David was even when facing what looked like a sure defeat? He was unafraid, because he knew who he was, and he knew that God was with him.

As the Philistine moved closer to attack him, David ran quickly toward the battle line to meet him (v. 48).

As his giant came closer and closer, David *ran* toward him. I don't know about you, but when I'm standing before a giant, I tend to run away. This is my initial instinct, until I realize that God is calling me to fight and defeat my giants. Only then can I move toward them with confidence. My trust isn't in my own strength but the power of Christ in me! When I surrender to Him, He makes it possible for me to accomplish things I could never take on alone.

As you read this story of David's tremendous courage, you might be thinking to yourself, *there's no way that could ever be me. I'm too _____. I'm not enough _____*.

Stop right there. The enemy may be telling you that you are too weak to face your giants, but it is time for you to realize your true identity and abandon those labels! You are a daughter of the King, and you are a mighty warrior.

MAKING THE EXCHANGE

In this chapter, we aren't taking a label off. We've already done that, and while God may continue to show you other labels that have defined your life and need to be removed, it is now time to put a new label *on*. That's right; this is one you'll want to wear proudly:

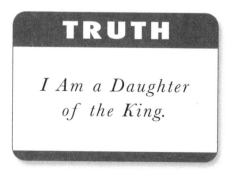

TRUTH

I Am a Daughter of the King.

You are not the sum total of
the words others have spoken over you.
You are not ugly; you are beautifully designed.
You are not a failure; you are more than enough.
You no longer have to live in shame;
you have been forgiven fully and are loved deeply.
You no longer have to strive to please others,
because your Father is well pleased with you.
Your value is not found in what you do
but who you are—a daughter of the King.
You are no longer broken; you have been made whole.
You are no longer rejected;
you have been accepted in Christ.

"I will be a Father to you, and you will be my sons and daughters, says the Lord Almighty." ~ 2 Corinthians 6:18

"You're sons of Light, daughters of Day. We live under wide open skies and know where we stand." ~ 1 Thessalonians 5:5, The Message

"I have told you these things, so that in me you may have peace. In this world you will have trouble. But take heart! I have overcome the world." ~ John 16:33

Download these Scriptures at
www.beautifullydesigned.com/PrintScriptures.

Next Steps

Though this book has come to an end, your journey has just begun. Now that you've learned how to abandon the labels that have held you back in exchange for God's truth, your next step is to *live brave* every day.

Perhaps you've been in church your entire life, or maybe this whole idea of a "relationship with God" is totally new for you. If you're just starting out this journey, your first step is surrender. And if you've been on this journey for some time, your next step is surrender as well.

When we surrender to God, we give up control of our lives and our attempts to try to make life work on our own. When we do this, we receive God's life and are filled with His fullness, which enables us to live brave, victorious, abundant lives.

It doesn't matter where you've been or what you've done. It doesn't matter if you don't pray very often and aren't quite sure how to begin a conversation with God. It doesn't even matter if you don't fully trust Him yet—just give Him a chance to show you how good and how faithful He is!

He knows your heart; He knows your thoughts; He knows your giants. Rise up, daughter, for you are His. You are accepted, loved, and have a glorious future ahead of you. There is no need to shrink back in shame or fear. There is nothing in your future that God is unprepared for, so there is no need to worry.

Whether you've been walking with God for fifty years or need to surrender to Him for the first time, I invite you to get on your knees and stretch your hands out in front of you, palms facing upward. As you open your hands, open your heart and say these words with me, *I surrender my life to You, Jesus. Help me to overcome to pain of my past and find my inner warrior so I can defeat the giants that surround me.* (List your giants and release your fears to God.) *"I ask for your strength as I go through this life and pray that you would reveal to me how deeply loved I am."*

Now, open your Bible to Psalm 139 and catch a further glimpse of His heart for you.

This is my favorite part:

I praise you because I am fearfully and wonderfully made; your works are wonderful, I know that fully well. My frame was not hidden from you when I was made in the secret place, when I was woven together in the depths of the earth. Your eyes saw my unformed body; all the days ordained for me were written in your book before one of them came to be (Psalm 139:14-16).

When you fully understand how uniquely you were designed, your beautiful destiny will begin to unfold. I don't know what season of life you are in, but I know every season has its struggles. In the midst of these struggles, it can be easy to forget your true identity—that you are royalty, God's daughter. This new label that you have put on will help you shine through the struggles and awaken your inner warrior.

If you don't know what to do or where to go from here, allow me to encourage you. When I was a young girl, my sister and I loved to play basketball outside. When it was time for dinner, Mom would stick her head out the door and yell, "Girls, get inside!" We knew her voice; it was the same voice that would sing to us while God wove us together in her womb, the voice that calmed us when we had nightmares, and the voice that sternly but lovingly corrected us when we disobeyed. Her voice was familiar, and as we grew older we learned

Next Steps

how to distinguish her tone, easily identifying the difference between when dinner was ready and when we were in trouble.

Do you know God's voice? Have you learned to distinguish it from all the other voices and noise in your life. If you desire to surrender to God and find your identity in Him, you have to *know* Him, and the more you get to know Him the easier it will be to recognize His voice.

Now that you have abandoned negative labels and discovered God's truth, it is time to create new habits so you can live out of your new identity and continue to discover who God says you are. The most practical of these habits is setting aside intentional time to draw near to God, discover who He is, and learn what His voice sounds like. Other habits may include silencing the negative voices in your head and the negative self-talk that you used to give into, surrounding yourself with more positive influences, or taking time to pray about things that make your heart restless instead of allowing worry and fear to overwhelm you.

As you close this book and go about your day, you will have many choices to make. These choices may involve what you will cook for dinner, where your next meeting is, how hard you will study for your next test, or how you will take care of your parents. There will be lots of things competing for your time and attention, but there is one thing that matters most. The Bible says if you draw near to God, He will draw near to you (James 4:8).

My prayer is that you will grow so close to God that you finally discover how much greatness He has put inside of you, and the negative labels that have defined your life begin to fade away as they are eclipsed by God's Truth.

I believe the best place to begin drawing closer to God is through the Scriptures. Even if it's only ten minutes a day, if you want to learn to recognize God's voice, start with reading the words He has already spoken. If you aren't sure where to begin, there are several Bible reading plans that can be found online. You can even start with the Scriptures from this book, which are available on the Beautifully Designed website (beautifullydesigned.com/PrintScriptures).

As we draw closer to God, it's also important to draw closer to one another. If you don't have a mentor, start praying for one! You never know who God will bring into your life. I have found there is great power in community. I am blessed to be a part of a small group that meets nearly every Wednesday night. We have women ranging in ages from twenty-four to seventy-eight. I love having so many different generations present, so we can encourage one another and share our own life experience with others. These ladies are my tribe; we laugh, cry, and pray together. The leader of the group, Janie Kennedy, has been a source of strength for me through many times of uncertainty.

The last thing I want to talk about is prayer. I used to pray like this: "Oh Jesus, thank you for the blessings in my life and keeping me healthy and safe." I knew how to throw in churchy words here and there to make it sound good. I quickly discovered that this type of prayer wasn't actually helping me grow in my relationship with God. Now, my prayer life looks a bit different. I'm free to be real and cry out to God when I need Him most. I understand that He knows my heart, because He is the one who created it. I talk to God like I would my husband or a mentor. I ask Him questions. I just asked Him how I should end this book, and felt Him whisper to remind each of you that He is always there for you, waiting for you to draw near to Him.

Precious daughters, God does not want you to sleepwalk through life, barely getting by. He wants you to live awake and aware of how deeply loved you are. He wants you to be courageous, to take risks, and allow Him to lead your journey. He wants to stay in constant communication with you and be involved in every area of your life.

We are each born with a void that only Christ can fill. As you close this book, I invite you to pick up your Bible and draw near to Him. Remember, your past mistakes, present circumstances, and the opinions of others do *not* define you. You are a daughter of the One who died for you and lives inside of you (and you will always have this book to remind you of that!). God is the only one who has the power to define you.

One last thing, don't forget your crown! All daughters of the King wear crowns.

"What is mankind that you are mindful of them, human beings that you care for them? You have made them a little lower than the angels and crowned them with glory and honor." ~ Psalm 8:4-5

Connect with Us

Our time has come to an end, but you are never alone. We want to stay connected to you through our Beautifully Designed community! This online community is made up of more than 17,000 women from all walks of life and backgrounds who come together regularly to pray, study the Scriptures, and give one another hope as each discovers their true identity in Christ. For direction on how to join the community, please visit www.beautifullydesigned.com/JoinCommunity.

If you would like to contact Ashley and the Beautifully Designed ministry team, you may do so at www.beautifullydesigned.com/contact. We love hearing how God is transforming lives through this ministry!

ACCEPTED CHRIST?

If you have made the decision to surrender your life to Jesus, or if you'd simply like to learn more about what this means, we invite you to visit beautifullydesigned.com/MeetJesus.

NEED PRAYER?

There are times when we all need prayer and support, and we are here for you! If you would like to receive prayer or speak to a member of our ministry team, you may reach out to us at beautifullydesigned.com/contact. You may also find it helpful to reach out to a local pastor, mentor, counselor, or trusted friend if you need ongoing care. We cannot live life alone!

Bring Ashley to Your Community

Whether you are planning a women's conference or gathering a small group, Ashley loves to speak to groups of all sizes and ages. Her communication style is marked by a down-to-earth tone and relatable transparency as she presents a message of hope for women in every season of life.

Ashley feels called to travel and communicate her God-given message to as many women as possible. If you would like to bring her to your community, we invite you to fill out the form at www.beautifullydesigned.com/speaking. No event is too large or too small!

About the Author

Ashley Shepherd is a wife, mother, entrepreneur, public speaker, published author, and minister to women. The daughter of a preacher, she was born and raised in Eastern Tennessee, where she lives today with her husband, Ryan, and their two boys, Wilson and Levi. In the fall of 2015, Ashley launched an online Bible study that quickly grew to more than 9,000 women in just four weeks. Today, the Beautifully Designed community is composed of over 17,000 women who regularly join together to pray, study the Scriptures, and give one another hope as each discovers their true identity in Christ.

Ashley is a graduate of Middle Tennessee State University and holds a degree in journalism. *Beautifully Designed* is her first book. Ashley is based near Knoxville, TN and is available to speak at conferences and women's events nationwide. You can learn more about her ministry at www.beautifullydesigned.com.

God is in the midst of her;
she shall not be moved;
God will help her when morning dawns.

~ Psalm 46:5, ESV